"From the dedication page to the v₤ celebrates being deep in the little m spinning too-muchness of being a N parents in my classes, as Brit's collection of stories and suggestions bring great understanding, reassurance, and humor to life with a toddler. One thing is true: The way to joy is through the exhaustion and chaos, and these prompts point the way. Bravo to Brit for creating something personal, beautiful, and REAL for mamas everywhere."

—KAREN DEERWESTER, owner of Family Time, Inc. and host of the *See Me Hear Me Love Me* podcast

"Ever since participating in Brit's take-a-break challenge in 2016, I've been a big fan of her work. Not only has she inspired various MOPS communities I've invited her to speak at, but thanks to her engaging and convincing principles on self-care, I've kept up with many habits I've developed from her online programs. Now, she has created a book for moms that is simple in practice yet so deeply powerful. Her writing is a gift."

—SHERRI CRANDALL, VP of Global Ministries and Leadership Experience at MOPS International

"I adore the format and heart behind *Mama Be Present*. It's not just a book. It's a beautiful memory keeper. We all buy baby books, but then they're just another thing on the to-do list that never gets done. Yet Brit's book is a great way for moms to capture memories while also doing something for their mental health. It's such an inspiration."

—MARY MCCONVILLE, artist, modern mom muse, and creator of Grow Up Brite Creations

"Not only is this a great book for toddler moms to remember that they're living some of their best memories, but as a mom of kids who now have their own kids, it was also impactful for me. I was smiling, laughing, reminiscing, and ultimately feeling at peace with being a mom."

—KAY BENESH, retired senior partner, Deloitte

FROM THE MAMA BE PRESENT COMMUNITY

"Brit strikes a powerful balance between hilarious and raw, story and research, and light-hearted and profound as she walks alongside moms guiding them in the most contradictory role in life: motherhood."

—CHRISTIN BOURG, mama and special education teacher

"I didn't realize how much I needed this until I read the last page with tears streaming down my face. It makes me feel so seen. Every time I read it, I discover new ways to connect with my kids and most of all, myself."

—ERIN MARTINEZ, mama and public health professional

"This is perfect for any mama. You can read a page or two to reset your day or mood or sit down and devour the whole thing. It's a book us moms can come back to over and over for the gentle reminders we ALL need."

—SARAH WOLL, mama and pilates coach

"Brit has helped me see that everyday seemingly insignificant things actually play a big role in creating joy. From ways to PLAY with my kids without embarrassment to how to plan for certain situations, this book has shifted my expectations and given me great tools for joyful parenting."

—KRISTAL SCHNEIDER, full-time mama

"I'm astonished at how thought-provoking *Mama Be Present* was for me. All along, you think it's just about how to be a more present mom, but in reality, you're also finding who YOU are again. I was in tears at the end. Brit's prompts are some of the most insightful things I've ever read. 'Stop. Drop. Mom.' and 'Return to You' will stay with me forever."

—AMY NORBERT MCKEON, mama and special education teacher

"Brit's examples of focused motherhood are so profound. Her book is like a complimenting friend on your shoulder."

—SARIAH DINCOLA, full-time mama

"This book will have you crying and laughing from start to finish. While Brit constantly reminds us how precious the early years are, she also offers genius tips and hilarious perspectives on the everyday struggles we can all relate to. It's such an inspiring toolkit for all moms."

—MIRNA TOMIC, mama and training and development manager

MAMA BE
PRESENT

40 SIMPLE YET MAGICAL WAYS
TO FIND JOY IN THE TODDLER DAYS

BRIT STUEVEN

ILLUSTRATIONS BY JERRY GEROU

- All illustrations by Jerry Gerou.
- Cover and interior design by Brit Stueven.
- Cover spine image by Kseniya Lapteva.
- Back cover copy by Eunice Brownlee.
- Image on page 18 by Xin & Xin Photography.
- Excerpt on page 117 from "Why We Long for the Most Difficult Days of Parenthood" by Stephanie H. Murray in *The Atlantic*. Reprinted by permission.
- Illustration on page 127 based on image by Edward Howell.

The following illustrations were based on images from these mamas (Thank you!):

- Sarah Woll, page 34 + 61
- Lisa Salzman, page 37
- Beret Finken, page 46 + 56
- Lana Effron, page 51
- Xin Zheng, page 103
- Kristal Schneider, page 129
- Kadra Brophy, page 136

Mama Be Present

This one's for you, tired, beautiful mama.

I hope this inspires you.

♡, Brit

BY THE

BOOK

BY THE

fill your cup

p-p-p-

THEME

show your love

play

how it began

One exceptionally tiring morning, my 3-year-old and I were sitting hip to hip on the couch eating apples. The TV was off, my phone was out of sight, and all you could hear was, well, apples. Then, he leaned in and kissed my cheek.

My world stopped spinning in the best way possible. My heart was flooded with everything that was missing. Then, I had an AHA:

> If something as simple as a mid-snack smooch can fill me up and make every challenge worth it, what else is possible?

As I started jotting down some of my favorite mamahood memories, I quickly noticed a theme:

The best moments were the simple ones.

The ones that lasted mere seconds. The ones that were painfully basic, such as:

- blowing a string back and forth between our faces and the laughter changing the vibe of a heavy morning.
- announcing bedtime with a paper towel roll and watching a mundane routine turn into something worth remembering.
- saying yes (for once!) to eating under the table with him and it suddenly changing everything: our conversation, how the food tasted, and more.

Here's something else I noticed at these joyful junctures:

In an instant, I was present.

Because of one small decision or single change of events, I went from tired to inspired...overwhelmed to overflowing...depleted to reignited. My heart was softened and open, my senses were fully awakened, and I was *paying attention.*

I realized that YES, this was the most intense season of my life to date, but it was ALSO the most beautiful. Even the hardest of days were dotted with small miracles. I just had to open my eyes to see them.

Then, I realized something that REALLY widened my eyes:

In eight months, JeeWoo would turn 4 and (Gasp!) no longer be a toddler. Suddenly, I was hit by a wave of grief and urgency.

You know how some nights you can't wait for your kid to be asleep, and the second they are, you miss them? That's how I felt in that moment.

As soon as I saw myself on the other side
of this all-consuming thing called toddlerhood,
I yearned for it. As soon as I saw these long,
tiring days slipping through my fingers,
I wanted to HOLD ON to them.

All at once, I wanted to seize this fleeting season with intention while also starting an honest conversation with other moms. I craved community and was curious if what was helpful for me was impactful for others.

I also had a deep desire to create on a regular basis. With that, I wanted accountability to share my writing every single week, whether I thought it was good enough or not. #doneisbetterthanperfect

Within a month, I created a Facebook group, Instagram page, rough content outline, and on February 1, 2022, **Mama Be Present** was born.

Every Tuesday, I posted a short story with a practical "joy prompt" on the MBP social media pages. And in between each prompt, there were relevant questions, quotes, or reminders.

Here's what I hoped for:

- By connecting more intentionally with their kid/s, even for a few minutes, moms would connect more with themselves.
- Through these simple nudges, they would see the hard days through a different lens or experience SOMEthing that helped them hang on.
- When they looked back on this time, these tiny moments would be the mightiest of memories.

Here's what I learned:

- While connecting with our kids can spark all kinds of day-changing, game-changing goodness, it's also vital to have some separation and space to recharge. Being connected with ourselves *first* is the BEST gift we can give to our children.
- The little things ARE the big things, and just minutes of pure connection can turn into something that's remembered forever.
- You don't have to be mega creative or super silly to make a kid's day. Sometimes, all you have to do is follow their lead.
- It's a bit of an oxymoron to send moms to social media (and only social media) for suggestions and reflections on being present.

So...

THAT is why I created a BOOK.

I wanted you to have a non-public, non-digital, oh-so-tangible place to do your own chronicling and capturing. I wanted you to have something you could hold and smell and sometimes write in while you drank your coffee, hid in the bathroom, had dinner on simmer, waited for school to get out, or whenever you needed a gentle nudge or encouraging reminder.

And then...

POOF! It happened. It's a THING. You're holding it. (Are you smelling it? Please smell it.)

Before you get your nose *too* deep into it, though, here's a quick rundown on what this is, what this isn't, and how best to use it.

Follow me, my friend. >>>

what this is

This book is for the mom who's seeking more joy in her life, but is too dang tired to even know where to begin.

It's for the mom who feels like...

...she's invisible.
...there's not enough time.
...she's the only one who loses it.

It's for the mom who feels "both...and..." about motherhood: completed and depleted. loved and suffocated. needed and lonely.

It's for the mom who wants to...

...wake up for alone time, but never gets to it.
...be the fun mom, but just can't play dolls or Hot Wheels again.
...pursue something for herself but has no idea what that is anymore.

It's for the mom who needs a safe place to document her toddler's darnedest and most inappropriate one-liners. #penis #poop #WTF

It's for the mom who is sometimes...

...jealous of bears in hibernation. #letmesleep
...dreaming of driving to California and, well, staying there.
...wishing her kid/s were older, then immediately feeling guilty.

If this is you, I see you.

Welcome to the jungle, my friend. In can be rough in here, but just think of all the moms who've made it out alive and now long to be *back* here. It's hard to see it now, but good things can happen here.

This book is a cozy campfire in the middle of the chaos.

By this fire, we share honest stories and roast fat marshmallows. We sip strong coffee and laugh till we pee a little. We share what we're learning and never forgetting, all while having faith in what we cannot see just yet.

In this corner of the wilderness, struggles are appreciated.
Guilt doesn't win. And most of all? Joy *is* possible.

what
this isn't

This book is not about cherishing every moment of motherhood.

It's about seeking *glimmers* of joy and beautiful flickers of connection, all while accepting that parenting is challenging and not always enjoyable.

"Not every day has to be good, and raising kids IS hard and often unpleasant. But when I think about the little things, I realize I DO love what I'm doing," said Beret Finken, a member of the Mama Be Present Community.

It's not a rainbows-and-butterflies approach to being present.

Just like play doesn't have to be silly or smiley, presence doesn't solely belong to the positive moments. It can also mean facing your feelings, being okay with not being okay, letting yourself cry in front of your child, and the like.

It means living life right now, whether it's wonderful, boring, or awful. It means seeing this season as a jigsaw puzzle and giving every piece of it a purpose. Some days will stand out and easily connect with joy, while some will feel impossible. With this book, we will trust that they all fit together.

It's not Pinterest-y, shiny, or wow-worthy.

None of these prompts will call for special tools, talents, or buying anything except maybe some glow sticks because GLOW STICKS. You might even roll your eyes at how simple, obvious, or basic some are. But here's the thing: The little things ARE the best things. And being present requires intention and a whole lotta reminders.

It's not a substitute for psychological or medical advice.

I'm not a licensed professional. I do, however, have a self-given doctorate in finding beauty in the most unexpected, overlooked things. I've also helped hundreds of people with their self-care, goals, and dreams. With that, I feel called to share what's helped me in hopes that it'll inspire you.

Before we start chatting and roasting our 'mallows, though, I see a few questions written all over your face:

What's this gal's story?
What makes her qualified to be my joy guide?

who we are

Well, hi! I'm Brit, and that handsome little dude is my son JeeWoo.

While my current title is stay-at-home mom (SAHM), which I think should stand for Selfless And Heroic Mama, I've worn many hats in this life: journalist, PR biz owner, golf course manager, self-care coach, and, and, and.

I'm a multi-passionate butterfly who had 19 part-time jobs and internships in college alone. I've taken plenty of leaps and pivots with no plans in sight. But 20 years later, I see that *everything* had a purpose.

Even long before entering motherhood, I led and mentored thousands of Family & Parenting writers at Examiner.com, helped many mom-facing companies with their marketing, and watched hundreds of mamas benefit from my programs on break-taking.

Then, as I waited...and waited...and waited to become that mom I always longed to be, I went through the darkest tunnel of my life. As I endured infertility and depression, I felt incapable in every way.

Yet deep in the wells of my woes and isolation, I found God again. I went to therapy. I got back on medication. I even paused my biz for a short gig at a golf course that turned into a two-year second *home*.

> **As glimmers of light shined back into my soul, I saw beauty in all of my pain and witnessed many a miracle in the smallest of things.**

Then, my husband David and I decided to embark on something we had always planned for: international adoption. We knew it wouldn't be easy, and boy, were we right. Our journey had hiccups and delays *every* single step of the way.

But by the grace of God and *the* most perfect timing, we brought our son home on October 28, 2020. After 24 months in the process and 52 nights in South Korea, JeeWoo Moon Stueven was finally here. We were elated and exhausted...amazed and terrified...grateful and clueless.

Thanks to training through our agency, we were prepared for him to have a heckuva transition. But little man did better than we did. (I mean, starting parenting with a 2-year-old in the middle of a pandemic right before winter is not for the faint of heart.)

They also told us, "There might be days when you look at each other and ask, 'What were we thinking?'"

"Pffft! Not me," I told D. "After everything we will have gone through, I can't see that happening. Even when he's screaming, I'll just be happy he's here with us."

Oh, my starry-eyed assumptions were right in line with those moms who say they'll never give their kid a pacifier, hand them a screen at a restaurant, or the other hundred things that go out the window when reality hits.

Let's just say that this long-awaited season — the one I wanted with every fiber of my being — has brought out sides of me I didn't know existed, all while filling me with unexplainable gratitude.

Motherhood is beautiful *and* confusing...wonderful *and* challenging. It's the most paradoxical thing I've ever experienced. But deep in the tension of those dualities is where we grow.

THE GREATER THE PAIN, THE MORE JOY YOU CAN CONTAIN. THE LONGER THE WAIT, THE BETTER IT TASTES.

A friend recently told me that because it was harder than usual for me to become a mom, I've been that much more capable of finding ways to be present. It brought tears to my eyes and sparked the same kind of urgency I felt when I realized his toddler days were slipping away. It made me wonder:

Was my desire to seize those remaining months also intensified from missing the first two years of his life?

It got me thinking about loss, and how even though it's difficult, it does have a way of helping us live harder. Grief gifts us an ever-expanding ability to experience things differently.

In fact, I believe that every struggle of every size is paired with a silver-lining of sorts. Take the other day, for example. After a rough night with J-Dub and an even tougher morning, a tiny miracle happened:

Crankenstein noticed a happy face in his muffin crumbs. It left us in awe and immediately lifted our moods. But had we not experienced those earlier challenges, would that edible emoji had brought us the level of joy that it did? I don't think so!

Speaking of joy, JeeWoo has been the best teacher on this topic. Why?

NO ONE KNOWS MORE ABOUT THE ART OF JOYFUL LIVING THAN A TODDLER.

Oh, how he LOVES running in circles, digging in dirt, spotting the moon, jumping in puddles, rolling down hills, unfolding umbrellas, rummaging through drawers, anything with sprinkles, anything that twinkles, and never leaving home without a spatula, whisk, or paper clip.

Without his willful spirit, attention to detail, and wondrous way of seeing the world, most of these prompts wouldn't exist. He's been the best little co-pilot this gal could ask for. A tiring one, yes, but one that challenges me, surprises me, and brings that crazy-good joy to me.

You see, sometimes all we need is right in front of us. And sometimes there are those days when we can't ask for help, make another decision, or make time for anything but surviving.

But just like turning on music when the sun is setting can immediately stop the sky from falling, I've found that a sliver of focused time with your little one can change everything.

It only takes one spark to re-light that fire, mama.

We're over the moon to journey with you,

Brit

JeeWoo

how to use this

Throughout this book, three main themes are at work:

Fill Your Cup • Show Your Love • P-P-P-Play

To me, these are the main ingredients of joyful parenting. As you'll find, however, they aren't broken into sections. When I polled moms on segmenting vs. blending the chapters, "mixed up" won because mom life is mixed up. And let's be real: If the fill-your-cup / self-care chapters had their own area, you and I both know we'd skip over it. But:

Sometimes you'll be seeking something specific.

One day, you'll need some emergency reprieve. (Psst! Turn to page 52 to stop. drop. and breathe.) Or one night, that bath-time transition will call for a trick. (Quick! Page 122!) Therefore, there are two tables of contents.

- "By The Book" shows everything in chronological order.
- "By The Theme" shows the joy prompts by topic.

If a prompt doesn't speak to you, make it YOURS!

But don't judge any chapters by their titles or ditch 'em before reading 'em. In the process of using your discretion on that irrelevant or "meh" suggestion, you just might have an AWESOME idea of your own.

If something flops, try it again.

Treat these ditties like anything that needs practice, like yoga or learning an instrument. It won't always be great, but the more you try it, the more chances you'll have to be changed or inspired by it.

Paint the walls any way you wish.

If you prefer not to write in it, that's okay! If you want to color the line art while answering questions in your head, go for it. If you want to fill every blank space with doodles and thoughts, they're waiting for you.

Use it when and where you want.

Whether you use this weekly, occasionally, or as a 40-day challenge, it's completely up to you. Keep it in your purse if you want. Stash it by your coffee maker. Heck! Put it in the bathroom. Long story short:

Pick your pace. Give yourself grace. Do what works for YOU in this space!

the days are long
but the years
are short

let's make
tiny, mighty
memories

shall we?

One of the most powerful ways to meet your child's basic desires and show them you love them is through the simple yet radical act of making eye contact.

SAY 'EYE' LOVE YOU

After a full day of driving here, running there, folding this, cleaning that, wiping butts, and cooking stat, we often hit the pillow wondering if it was enough. Even after ALL the things we did with our invisible capes on, we can't help but feel guilty over what we did or didn't do.

I didn't play with him enough. I was on my phone too much. She had chicken nuggets AGAIN. I yelled too many times.

Then, our inner Jesse Spano* screams, "There's no time! There's never any tiiime!"

But maybe more time isn't what we need. Perhaps a shift in HOW we spend our time is key. In other words, it's time to give ourselves grace. We think if we're not going big with everything, we're failing. But guess what?

THE THINGS OUR KIDS NEED THE MOST FROM US ARE THE THINGS THAT DON'T ASK MUCH OF US.

One of the most powerful ways to meet your child's basic desires AND show them you love them is through the simple yet radical act of making eye contact.

By locking eyes with your little one — specifically in those in-between, playful moments — you're communicating in more ways than you think. You're saying, "I'm here. I'm interested. I love you."

And this might blow your mind: Researchers at the University of Cambridge and Nanyang Technological University in Singapore found that when moms and babies were making eye contact, their brain waves were in sync![1]

If that's not motivation to slow down and crouch down with your little love sponge, I don't know what is.

---

*Didn't grow up in the 90s? This is referencing an unforgettable "Saved By The Bell" scene where after becoming addicted to caffeine pills to be the perfect student, Jessie has an epic meltdown.

Here are some ideas to gently spark the connection:

- Have a staring contest.
- Play a game of Peek-a-boo.
- Invite them to sit in your lap.
- Sit across from them during a meal.
- Join them while they're playing. Start asking questions.
- Ask them if they want a happy face drawn on their hand.
- When parked or at a red light, turn around and give 'em a funny face OR move to the music while looking at them.

If your tiny tornado doesn't look at you or give in, all is not lost. Just the *intention* of making eye contact might make you more present. It sure softens me on those really hard days!

So, mama. Are you ready to melt into the moment with your child?

GO AHEAD. SAY EYE LOVE YOU.

recap How'd it go? Describe the scenario. Any surprises or increase in connection?

remember What's one of your most vivid memories involving eye contact? Why do you think it has stuck with you?

**YOU'RE NOT
A BAD MOM.**

**YOU'RE PROBABLY
JUST DEHYDRATED.**

MAMA BE NOURISHED 2

Pictured on Instagram: *JeeWoo and I enjoying a fishing adventure on a boat with friends.*

Not Pictured: *He and I having epic, post-ride, public meltdowns in the parking lot.*

Over the course of four hours, we didn't eat or drink enough (Hi, pontoon boat with no toilet!), he woke up 10x the night before (He'll never go to bed with a toilet paper roll again!), and I was hungover. So, he and I were already on edge.

Then, in typical toddler fashion, he wasn't ready to leave. He wanted one more minute on a bench with this golden statue man. I didn't have patience for timers or negotiating. Everyone was leaving. I was driving one of the cars. We had to go.

As I picked up Ticking Time Bomb, he completely exploded and continued to...all the way up the hill...in the blaring sun...arms and legs flailing...screaming and wailing...with EVERYONE staring. Then:

Thanks to plummeting blood sugar, 36 pounds of flapping flesh in my arms, and an extra-heavy bag on my back, it was the perfect storm for my own meltdown.

As he refused to be strapped into his car seat, I started crying and very loudly screamed, "STOP IT!!!"

Ugh. I felt horrible. Thankfully, my two girlfriends followed me and helped, but one of them had to embarrassingly drive for me. I was a complete mess. I don't know how many times I apologized.

At that particular moment, I felt like the only mom who had ever lost her sh*t in that way.

Us mamas FEEL LIKE we're the only ones.

We FEEL LIKE our kid is the only one who completely explodes like this. We FEEL LIKE we're the only ones who don't know what we're doing...

...*especially* when most of what we see on social media or discuss at a playdate is the polished stuff. But here's a reminder about the un-pictured and sometimes shameful moments in parenting:

WHEN THINGS GO SOUTH, IT'S PROBABLY BECAUSE OUR BASIC NEEDS AREN'T BEING MET.

In those messy moments, you're not a terrible mother or the "only one." You're a normal human who is likely one or more of the following:

- hungry.
- dehydrated.
- overwhelmed.
- sleep-deprived.
- overstimulated.

Or maybe something deeper is stirring.

While the root cause of many of my meltdowns has been from some form of malnourishment, I can now look back and pin other things to them like grief, anxiety, hormones, depression, and the like.

No matter how big or basic the root of it's been, though, here are some things that have always helped after a good 'ol mama tantrum:

FEEL IT + FACE IT

Perhaps put your hand over your heart, take a breath, and ask yourself what's been missing. Hide in the bathroom if you have to. Bust out the Play-Doh or whatever will get you and your kiddo/s in a situation where you can reflect and breathe.

Maybe write about it. Angry-journal about it. (Don't want anyone to find it? Shred it. Burn it. Just get it OUT.) Name the emotion/s you're feeling while you're at it. Sit with it. See it. Feel it.

APOLOGIZE

One day, I said, "JeeWoo, I'm sorry I'm a Crankenstein. I'm SO tired. But I love you SO much." He laughed and gave me the biggest hug. Not only was it therapeutic for us both, but it sure lightened the morning routine.

TALK ABOUT IT

Let your partner/spouse know about it, tell other moms about it, or talk with a therapist about it. This will do at LEAST two things:

- **You'll learn you're not alone.** Every time I've confessed a "mom rage" moment to someone, I've always been met with a "Me too!!"
- **It'll allow for new perspectives.** When I told David about a *different* time I screamed at JeeWoo, it helped us both realize how burnt out I was. That weekend, he booked me a night at a hotel.

But a 24-hour getaway isn't always realistic, and we don't always need go-big-or-go-home methods to get recharged. What we often need is to get back to the basics. So...

KEEP IT SIMPLE

Pick ONE basic need that's been ignored lately and write it below.

_____

MAKE IT POSSIBLE

If it's hydration, keep a water bottle by your side or add something to it that will make you WANT it. (Lemon? Mint? A Nuun tablet?) If it's exercise, ditch "ideal" scenarios. Dance HARD for 10 minutes with your kid. Do jumping jacks in your PJs. Do a plank during bath time. Get my drift?

What's ONE simple way you'll make your basic need possible today? Write it below. Then, see what happens...

_____

JUST SAY YES 3

In the classic children's book *No, David!*, a mischievous little boy is told "No" left and right.

As he jumps on his bed with cowboy boots on, bangs pots and pans, and swings his bat in the living room, he hears things like, "Settle down!" "David! Be quiet!" "Not in the house, David!"

At the end, his mom wraps him in her arms as she says, "Yes, David...I love you!"

We say no to our little ones a lot. It's our way of protecting, teaching, and ultimately loving them. But how many times throughout the day are we declining their requests because we feel inconvenienced in some way?

What if, for once, we agreed to splash the bath water, climb into the fort, or let them make that mess? Could something game-changing spark from spontaneously saying yes?

One morning, JeeWoo wanted to sit on the counter while he drank his juice. Normally, I say no so I can do things around the kitchen and not worry about him breaking his legs. But on that day, I obliged and stayed close.

He immediately reached for the box of rocks I forgot to put back in my nightstand. (Yes. I have a collection of smooth pebbles from Greece that he brings out about 40x a week.)

Before I knew it, his bare, dirty feet and my beloved, beachy treasures were all over the counter. My patience was running dry.

Then, I remembered a "Wash the Toys" post I saw on Instagram from Susie Allison of Busy Toddler (@busytoddler). It basically shows the keep-em-focused power of a bin filled with toys and soapy water.

"Hey, buddy, do you want to wash those rocks and make 'em all shiny?" I asked.

"YEAAAAAHHH!" he yelled.

Not long after he got his hands into a suds-filled tupperware, he stood up and opened the cabinet where we keep his stuff.

"How 'bout blue cup? How 'bout green bowl?" he asked, as he reached for all the things.

"Sure! Yes! Whatever you'd like," I said.

Although I cringed over everything he got out, I sure loved how lit up he was. He eventually spilled so much water that it was dripping to the floor. Oh, but the JOY he felt!

This activity was so riveting, he later chose it over watching *Cocomelon*. (!!!) And although his feet were all over the countertop, I unloaded the dishes and made lunch *not* to the sounds of Netflix for once.

We were focused on different things, but we were close in proximity, and I could feel how much he appreciated that.

IT WAS A WELCOMED CHANGE OF PACE THAT FILLED US BOTH UP.

He didn't even fight his nap, later. I didn't even have to set a warning timer! Like, what?

In the days that followed, he asked me to find rocks in soap with him so much, it almost became annoying. But...

Look what transpired from adventurously saying, "Absolutely!"

So, the next time your little rebel has something crazy (but safe!) up their sleeve (Mismatching shoes? Pancakes for dinner? ANOTHER treat for the dogs?), hold back that nay and you WILL make their day.

Just say YES!

recap

What did you say yes to? Did the world end?
What sparked from a little bit of letting go?

These days, you may feel like you're achieving *nothing* or like no one's noticing.

Oh, but mama...

These are the days that you're someone else's *everything*.

SEE YOUR SEEDS 4

One of the hardest parts about becoming a mom was how invisible I felt. I had no idea how much I thrived off of being recognized and thanked for things...until I wasn't.

But through all the folding of laundry, cleaning of messes, stacking of Legos, digging in dirt, and [insert all those mind-numbing activities that actually allow us to reflect here], I've realized that:

- God always sees me.
- I'm not alone in this feeling. (I've asked SO many moms.)
- SO much of what's essential is also invisible. In other words:

Some of the most vital things in this world — oxygen, electricity, atoms, gravity, plumbing — often go unseen.

Even things like our feelings, memories, and emotions are unseeable. We can see the effects of them, of course, and we can put them into words, art, or actions, but their sheer essence is intangible.

You know what all these things have in common?

THEY'RE INVISIBLE *AND* INVINCIBLE.
THEY HAVE AN UNDENIABLE POWER.

And how often do you think *they* are getting thanked? Do *you* ever stop and show gratitude to the lights in your home? How often do you toss a "Gracias" to the gravity beneath your feet? I've never thought to do such a thing, yet I am SO grateful for these things.

Therefore, just because something goes unnoticed or unacknowledged, it doesn't mean its purpose isn't paramount.

So, if these days, you feel like you're achieving nothing or feel like no one's noticing, just remember:

These are the days that you are someone else's everything.

Being the electricity of the family is a force to be reckoned with. Your ripples are more powerful than you think.

Just like Mother Theresa said:

"If you want to change the world, go home and love your family."

Your love is a superpower.

It's not the type of power that lets you make things disappear with the twitch of your nose. It's actually the complete opposite. It's so slow-cooked, you won't even witness its full effect in this lifetime.

But please trust that every second of your attention and compassion for your child/ren is making a difference, whether you see it today or not.

So, what "invisible" things have you been doing that have actually been planting world-changing, legacy-leaving, life-molding seeds?

We're talking things like:

*morning cuddles / listening / smiles / laughing / playing
eye contact / hugs at drop-off / consistent meals
2am cuddles / snacks / letting them see you cry*

Write them on the next page.
See your seeds, mama.

There are only two places
I haven't taken my phone
with me:

1) the shower
2) the ocean

HIDE YOUR PHONE 5

Whenever I can't find my phone or I forget it at home, it feels like my arm was cut off. I treat the thing like it's a body part, and I know I'm not the only one.

I also know this topic isn't new to you. Unless you're an elephant or live in an igloo, you've heard about tech addiction or seen a "Put Your Phone Down" meme by now.

But here's something that might be new to you:

Simply putting your phone down isn't enough. The mere presence of it not only tempts you to grab it more, but it also affects your attention.

A 2017 study from the McCombs School of Business at the University of Texas at Austin found that when a smartphone is close by, it reduces our ability to focus.

When close to 800 people were tested on how well they could complete computer tasks with smartphones nearby, those with their phones in the other room performed much better than those with their phones on the desk and slightly better than those who stashed it in their pocket/bag.[1]

They also found that it doesn't matter if it's face down or turned off. When the brain tries not to focus on something, it's still focusing in some capacity — therefore draining mental energy.

So, if you want to be fully present with your child/ren and totally free of distraction, then here's your plan of action:

STASH THAT TELE!

Pick one time today to banish your phone for at least 30 minutes. Perhaps set a timer. Maybe...

- Leave it on your nightstand after you wake up.
- Place it in a completely different room.
- Stash it in a kitchen drawer.
- Leave it in your car.

Whatever you do, get it out of sight, out of mind, and most certainly on silent before you hide it.

Feeling extra brave? Hide it right now.

recap

How did cutting off your arm feel? (Har!)
Where'd you hide it? What came of it?

remember

List three times you were so engrossed in the moment you didn't even think to feast your eyes on your phone.

Do more things that make you forget to check your phone.

JUST ROLL WITH IT 6

Is today a day that's going awry?
Are you so burnt out you're too tired to cry?
Did your toddler wake up two hours too soon?
Are they screaming again for that red balloon?

Well, now that whole bag of berries just spilled.
And where is that third cup of coffee you filled?
Ah-ha! Next to that toast they won't eat.
Oh crap, now a poop-covered toilet seat.

Wherever you're at in this chaotic day,
Here's something that might melt your worries away:
First, remember you're far from alone,
If your house ain't a mess, it's not a true home.

Then, grab your kiddo and pump up the music,
Let go of perfection and just ROLL with it!

Dance in the kitchen,
Shake off your stress,
Spin 'round in circles,
Delay getting dressed.

Feel your moods lift,
As you let loose together,
And remember,
These moments,
They won't last forever.

The stressful, the blissful,
The heavy, the tender,
The ugly, the beautiful,
No, they won't last forever.

MUSIC.
CHANGES.
EV.ER.Y.THING.

So, music makes everything better — even the craziest morning at home with a toddler. Here's why:

It syncs with our body. Literally.

Minutes after a song comes on, our brainwaves, breath rates, and heart rates will sync to the beat. This process, called entrainment, was accidentally discovered in 1666 by Dutch scientist Christian Huyghen. While sick in bed, he noticed that the two pendulum clocks in his room eventually lined up their ticking.[1]

Ain't no mama got time to read the physics on how, but let's just say it comes down to sound energy. THIS is why music can so quickly change your mood!

It's also memory-boosting.

Not only does it help create memories (I'll never forget all the dancing we did in the kitchen when I was growing up!), but it helps us learn and remember things. Um, hello, "ABC song", and every piece of music that's brought us back to certain moments.[2]

But wait! There's more!

According to THE most informative Instagram post I've ever seen from @flourishinghomesandfamilies, (Dr. David and Amanda Erickson are amazing!) dancing with your kid/s can also:

- reduce stress.
- improve literacy.
- help heal trauma.
- enhance bonding.
- reduce depression.
- regulate emotions.
- release endorphins.
- boost concentration.
- increase self-esteem.[2]

A family dance party is definitely happening in our house tonight.

How about yours?

7 STOP. DROP. MOM.

I don't know what it is about dogs and small children, but their someone's-on-the-floor radar is impressive. Of course, they have no idea you exist when you ask them to go potty, keep walking, stay off that lawn, come inside, and, and, and...

BUT.

As soon as you're sitting or lying on the ground, they drop everything they're doing and attack...without warning...with all the playful love in the world. Pretty sure that and the pantry opening are the only two things that *actually* get their attention.

They're not the only ones who struggle to be pulled from their personal vortices, though. If we flipped the perspective, I'm sure toddlers would say that us mamas are just as hard to crack — especially when we're reading, texting, typing, cooking, cleaning, or participating in those things that toddlers are *made* to destruct: adult conversations.

Obviously, we can't give our kids the kind of attention they vie for 24/7. And of course, we still find ways to feel guilty about that, but, um, no one would survive.

Speaking of survival:

> Maybe you're wondering right this very second
> how you'll make it through today. Or maybe
> you know that feeling is inevitably on
> the way, because, well, parenting.

Maybe you need a quick breather or excuse to be silly with your kiddie. Wherever you stand, this might give you life again...

STOP what you're doing,
DROP to the floor, and be the
MOM they need right now.

This could mean:

- Grabbing your kiddo and playfully dropping to the floor together.
- Stop-drop-momming in the near distance and seeing how long it takes for your little magnet to come running.
- Spontaneously lying down next to them while they play.

Maybe they'll tackle you, sit on your stomach (or STEP on it!), lie next to you, or lay a thousand kisses on you. Perhaps they'll want nothing to do with this "being still" nonsense and lend a swift invite to play cars or Barbies.

Whatever their response is, roll with it. Melt into the moment with it.

8 STOP. DROP. BREATHE.

With the last prompt, you were nudged to get on the ground with your toddler. This time, you're encouraged to lie down on the floor...all by yourself.

That's right, mama. Seek out a mini, solo savasana. And whatever you do, don't wait for the perfect scenario.

- Plop down in the closet if you have to.
- Sprawl out in the hallway during nap time.
- Sneak in a lie-down while they're in a Lego zone.
- Take five on the kitchen floor while they watch a show.

Worried about dirt? Slide something under your head. Is your mind racing with to-dos? Give 'em the finger while you let yourself linger.

If you get interrupted, let it flow. Let all the sounds, sights, or touches be part of this imperfectly perfect moment in time.

And with every fiber in your body...

SHIFT YOUR FOCUS INWARD
AND DO NOTHING ELSE
BUT B-R-E-A-T-H-E.

Then, watch this small break work some serious wonders.

According to psychotherapist and yoga teacher Ling Beisecker, when you're lying on the ground, your mind tends to focus on the inner workings of your body. Automatic, unconscious processes like breathing and heartbeat start to become conscious. This process, called interoception, is not only calming, but it can also decrease symptoms of anxiety and depression.[1]

If that's not enough motivation to get flat stat, savasana can ALSO:

- reduce stress.
- improve sleep.
- decrease fatigue.
- relieve a headache.
- lower blood pressure.[1]

And lying down on a hard, flat surface (Couches and beds don't count!) is also amazing for your muscles and bones. Your spine can realign to its natural posture while your back and neck muscles can finally catch a break from holding your body up.

IF you feel restless or anxious, it's OKAY. That's NORMAL. Let your thoughts bounce around exactly as they are. Simply focus on the rising and falling of those amazing lungs of yours, and remember:

When stress or fear hits, deep breaths are one of your most powerful, accessible tools to calm down.

So, the next time you need some emergency reprieve, don't delay.

STOP.
DROP.
BREATHE.

Not at home?
Don't forget that you can put the seat back in your car. #lifechanging

Not in a car?
No matter where you are or what you're doing, you can always focus on your breath. Feel it seep in and out of your body until you can *taste* the stillness.

Also. There's a reason people
jet at the end of yoga class.

Yes, lying like a corpse is
undeniably the easiest
pose ever, but it's also
the hardest to master.

It can be terrifying to sit with
your thoughts and actually
feel your emotions.

It can be frightening
to finally. be. still.

And to *stay* still.

But...

Sometimes doing nothing is the best way to move forward.

GREET 'EM GRINNING 9

Do you ever pick your kid up somewhere and they don't greet you the way you expected?

After being apart, you picture them running to you with the biggest smile and open arms, but instead, they shoot you a quick glance and get back to that toy. Or maybe they don't even acknowledge you at all.

Sometimes, it's a real punch in the gut, and lately, it's gotten me wondering:

How many times has JeeWoo approached me excitedly — especially in the morning — and not received the greeting he expected?

Well, given that his mom is part bear, could use a WEEK to prepare for every day ahead, thrives when she's alone, and is just now adjusting to his 6 a.m. wake-ups that kicked off two months ago, that number's probably pretty high.

And THAT is a real bummer for this innocent, little guy.

So, I've been making a point to change that. No matter how hard it is to lift the corners of my mouth some days, I do it — and I do it BIG.

I greet that day-starting darling with the biggest smile I can muster before he preps to flail something over the railing. From Giraffe to his shirt to a fresh pair of underwear, I never know what I'm gonna catch.

But here's what I do know: Seconds after I hang an intentional grin on my face, my frustration melts away, my focus hones in on him, and I'm genuinely ready to give him a huge hug, floor cuddle, or whatever he needs at that moment.

From there, there's this crazy ripple effect of joy. Of course, not every morning is rainbows + butterflies after I decide to smile (HA! If only it were that easy!), but there really is something to this.

Not only are smiles contagious, but they spur a chemical reaction in the brain that increases happiness and reduces stress.[1]

Also. The more aware I've become of my facial expressions, the more conscious I've been about how I act with him in other scenarios. It's been making me more present.

So, when your kid comes barreling outta their room or interrupting your work / convo / down time too soon, give 'em what *you* would expect and what they most certainly deserve:

THE. BIGGEST. SMILE.

recap

There *will* be unseen ripple effects from this big-little smiling thing. But what are you noticing within you? ...your kid/s?

remember

Who has made YOU feel seen and welcomed in your life because they always greeted you grinning?

WE SHALL NEVER
KNOW ALL THE GOOD
THAT A SIMPLE
SMILE
CAN DO

MOTHER THERESA

10 LET 'EM HELP

One morning, it was only 7:30 a.m., and I already needed space from my sticky, 3-foot shadow. Not only did he wake up 45 minutes earlier than expected AND before I even had one sip of coffee (GASP!), but after breakfast he was following me ev.er.y.where.

As I was trying to empty the dishwasher, JeeWoo kept getting in my way. He also kept asking me to play...over and over.

"Buddy, mommy needs to do the dishes, then I'm all yours, okay?"
"Okay," he said. But he kept standing there.

The kid just wants to be next to you. Let him be with you, something nudged me from within. *Maybe ask him where things go.*

It had been a long time since we played that little memory game with our kitchen items, so I kicked it off. He. was. so. excited.

Hearing the joy in his voice when he pointed to where things belonged was so energizing. With each placement, I felt more at ease.

When that was finished, I asked if he wanted to help me fill up the dish soap dispenser. He screamed like I had just told him he won a trip to the North Pole.

With each painfully simple step of refilling the soap, his amazement was hilarious. I mean, all I did was say, "Now, we take the lid off," and he was like, "Wait, WHAT?!"

When I asked him to come with me to put the bottle back in the laundry room, he was so pumped. And when I started running there? Oh, you KNOW he followed suit. Toddlers LOVE a prompt pursuit.

It's incredible how quickly that whole scenario changed, all thanks to a nudge to turn a mundane task into a moment of connection.

So, whenever you find yourself unraveling and your little one ain't skedaddling, perhaps there's a reason for it. Maybe there's a chance to make the most of it. Or maybe there's something you don't involve your toddler in (baking? cleaning? yard work?) that could actually be an opportunity for learning and connection.

Next time, let them help. Not only will they feel more connected to you and learn basic life skills, but when they finally nap or go to bed tonight, you'll have one less thing to tackle and more time to REST.

According to my toddler,
tears come from Home Depot
buckets, he doesn't have a butt
crack, and Santa is the president.

ASK THY TODDLER 11

When you have a toddler, there's no reason to pay for a comedy show. All you have to do is ask them certain questions and their wildly inaccurate yet oh-so-confident answers will have you dying of laughter.

To catch their full attention, I suggest announcing this and making it big for them. "JeeWoo! Please join me at the table, kind sir. I have some VERY important questions for you!"

Then, grab a pen and get ready to document GOLD. Ready, go!

Where do tears come from?

Why do we have butt cracks?

Who is the president?

When we flush a toilet, where does it go?

How old am I?

What makes you happy?

What's the funniest thing you've ever seen?

If you were 50 feet tall, what would you do?

What are you thankful for?

Where do babies come from?

Where does the sun go at night?

nothing CAPTURES THE MIND

LIKE SOMETHING unexpected

GLASS CANVAS 12

I'll never forget the time my dad invited me to trace the moon with Crayola markers on the window with him.

How is it that for nearly 30 years, these tiny, turquoise circles haven't escaped my brain? How is it that something that lasted maybe six minutes has remained etched in my mind's eye?

In 2018, the Happiness Research Institute conducted the Happy Memory Study, which prompted 1,000+ people of all ages and genders from 75 countries to describe one happy memory.

From wedding day stories to their child's first steps, some memories were big. Others captured the simple things, like watching soccer with their dad or eating cheese and pickle sandwiches.[1]

Of all the memories that were submitted, 100% contained something that was truly noticed or paid attention to.

Here's what else they found:

- 62% engaged the senses.
- 56% invoked emotion.
- 37% were meaningful.
- 23% harnessed the power of firsts.[1]

So THAT's why I remember that slice of time with my pops!

Also, most of what we did together in my childhood was sporty (shooting hoops, riding bikes, going to basketball games), so, when he prompted us to do something creative, he had my full attention.

Nothing captures the mind like something unexpected, and nothing activates a child's senses like freely drawing on a see-through, normally off-limits surface — especially for the first time.

So, are you plum out of ideas for the kiddos?

Well, my indoor innovator, it's time to turn an everyday, overlooked object (a window!) into an extraordinary opportunity (a glass canvas!).

**Get your hands on a dry-erase marker,
beeline to the nearest strip 'o glass,
and start doodling or drawing.**

Let your imaginations run wild.

Psst! Want to surprise them even MORE?

When they're not around, plant a simple drawing on the car window where they sit. Perhaps draw a heart, star, robot, or whatever your little one would fancy. See what happens.

recap

Did ya try it? How'd it go?

remember

Did this chapter bring up any of your own vivid memories?

13 HIDE A LOVE NOTE

When my dear pal Lana was young, her pops would put uplifting Post-its around the house for her. Not only were they hugely helpful after kids weren't nice at school, but this extremely small gesture continues to make an impact on her life today.

Those little notes of encouragement are now the basis of everything she creates through Lana's Shop, a custom illustration boutique.

Her biz motto is even "Nice matters," and the idea is that something handwritten, kind, and full of love could change someone's day.

Or what about be inked in their hearts forever?

Lana still has some of those Post-its hanging in her studio to this day, and I, too, have saved penned mementos from back in the day. From every card my mom mailed to me in college (and beyond!), to letters I asked my grandparents to write, to basically *any* encouraging words ever put to paper...yep! Still got 'em.

Wondering how these loving notes could translate for humans who can't read yet (What's up, toddlers?), I once tried an experiment.

While JeeWoo was napping, I drew a heart on five Post-its and placed them around the house.

Some were obvious. (Hello, kitchen table and bathroom mirror!)
Some were hidden. (Oh hey, jack-in-the-box lid!)
But here's what ALL of them had in common:

They were SO fun to hide. And...

FOR THE FIRST TIME EVER,
I COULDN'T WAIT FOR HIM TO WAKE UP.

When JeeWoo finally came blowing through, his reaction to the first one was priceless.

"Look! Mom! Valentine! Ohhhh, mom! JeeWoo keep it?"
"Of course," I said laughing.
"Ohhh," he said, as he smashed it against his cheek like a new teddy bear. "Mom, I love you so much."

I melted. A paper square with a basic heart that took all of two seconds to make...did THAT. And as the afternoon progressed, so did the excitement as he discovered his big, little treasures.

He loved it.
I loved watching it.
I *totes* recommend love notes.

A paper square with a basic heart that took all of two seconds to make ...did THAT.

14 A LOVE NOTE TO YOU

This exercise reminds me of when my therapist would have me look at a chair, pretend it was someone else, and, well, talk to it. It's weird, uncomfy, and maybe a little cheesy.

BUT.

Don't knock it till ya try it. There's a reason I'm nudging you to do this. And anything with cheese is worth trying, am I right?

On the next page, write a love letter to yourself. Pour some serious adoration on the incredible human and amazing mom that you are.

Need help getting that loving word train moving?

Here are some questions to ponder:

- What have you learned about yourself in this season?
- What have you done a dang good job with?
- What do you forgive yourself for?
- Is there something you're ready to let go of?
- What about something you want to start or change? Have you been too hard on yourself? Can you give yourself grace?

While you're writing this doting ditty, be sure to address yourself by "you" and/or your name. Why?

Studies show that when we talk to ourselves using "you" (You can do this!) instead of "I" (I can't!), it creates a safe distance between ourselves that allows us to be more self-compassionate.[1]

In other words, write to yourself as you would to a friend, and watch what transpires from this simple act of self-love.

I love the smell of possibility in the morning.

WAKE UP FIRST 15

This is not the first time you've been encouraged to "wake up first."

Not only is it as typical to see this in a mom-advice article as it is for an older mom to tell you to "Cherish every second," but any woman who's mastered the art of awakening before her family will tell ev.er.y.one. about it.

It can get annoying — especially when you're struggling just to *open* your eyes when your kid wakes *you* up or you're going through a rough sleep phase. I mean, after JeeWoo has screamed and cried three to five times in one night, the last thing I feel capable of is seizing the morning.

But now that I've gotten a solid taste of that oh-so-coveted quiet time, I understand why moms shout this from the rooftops. It *works.*

Waking up first is literally life-changing.

When you're the early bird, you can tackle what YOU need and what YOU want before anything unpredictable strikes. You can chip away at those things that creep into your daydreams. You can be YOU again.

You can drink your coffee HOT. You can eat uninterrupted. You can finally reply to things. You can actually *read*. You can work out untouched.

Not only are you able to put your oxygen mask on first, but you have time to breathe slowly...and richly...and truly charge your battery. And if you're highly sensitive to touch and sound, there's nothing better than starting the day surrounded by *quiet.*

Also. If you're susceptible to nighttime demons like I am (I have SO much self-doubt and overthink everything when it's dark!), it's to your utmost benefit to keep all things creative or self-reflective for the a.m. You'll be more productive and confident when you're fresh and rested.

Are you salivating for a delicious, soulful morning but it feels out of reach? Here's what's helped me:

- **Go slowly with your alarm.** Don't go balls to the wall at first. Inch your way in. Set your alarm 10 minutes earlier each day. Just those 10 extra minutes alone could do wonders!

- **Team up.** Get your spouse/partner on board if you can. When we head to bed at the same time and wake up at the same time, it holds us accountable on many fronts.

- **Get sober sleep.** Every time I drink, no matter how much, I can't get going the next morning. Alcohol affects your sleep big-time.

- **Have a specific goal or plan.** When I know exactly what I'm going to do, I'm more driven to get my butt out of bed. (Glennon Doyle used to wake up at 4:30 a.m. and hide in her closet to write!)

- **Just sit up and go.** Don't overcomplicate it. The sooner you get moving, the faster you'll wake up. And if you know what's good for you, you'll drink a full glass of water while you're at.

But what if you need the extra sleep?

If you're in a tough sleep stretch, sick, or whatever is keeping you up, don't force it. Listen to your body. Get those extra Zs!

When the kiddo awakes, kick your mom guilt to the curb and give 'em a show or three. Sometimes, if JeeWoo wakes at 6, he gets an hour of TV, and I'm a better mom because of it.

And what if you're not a morning person?

Everyone has different rhythms. Don't force this either if the evening is where you thrive.

Here's what I'll say, though: I *never* thought I was a morning person. Then, I cut out alcohol, and THAT sure changed. Many things changed, actually. (More in the next prompt.)

Before you move on, how about some rise-and-shine accountability for tomorrow? You are much more likely to accomplish something if you put it in writing, so let's get those morning plans DOWN!

What time will you wake up?

What will you do tonight to make tmrw happen?

What do you plan to do?

What's Plan B if Plan A flops because toddler?

How'd it go?

Any takeaways for next time?

16 MAMA BE SOBER

On April 10, 2022, I accomplished something quite big for me:

I made it 100 days without alcohol.

I wasn't sliding down rainbows or bursting with energy by that point, but I was waking up at 6 a.m. nearly every day and loving the space to create and write. I was more calm, confident, clear-headed, and most of all, more patient and present with JeeWoo.

Four days later, I broke my streak. Why?

In this season, it's hard not to "reward" myself with wine at the end of the day. I love sipping it while I cook. I love how it relaxes my every muscle, slows my anxious brain, and softens my overstimulated senses. I love the conversations it sparks with David.

Society tells me this is all normal. It's self-care for exhausted moms. It's our elixir for survival. #mommyjuice

But when morning hits, my body whispers different messages to my tired soul.

While I'm fighting through the fog, feeling irritable, and wishing I had the energy of my toddler, I tell myself, *Tonight will be a Topo Chico night.*

Then 5 p.m. hits, and so does my craving to be a little bit numb again.

The cycle continues. One glass turns into two or three, and then comes the whiskey. One night a week turns into every night, and before I know it, the thing that's "de-stressing" me is controlling me and unknowingly seeping into everything.

Three months after I broke my streak, I tried going easier on myself with Dry August. But *that* month brought a wrath of events that were so stressful it was almost comical. I didn't even last a week.

Then, life got even craaazier, so my nightly imbibing continued.

BUT.

As I write this, I'm on day 30 of another streak, and it feels GOOD. I've been waking up at 6 again, cranking away at something I've ALWAYS wanted to do (write a book!), feeling more calm and present again, and, and, and. Everything is better. *Everything*.

> **If this is pulling at anything within you, I strongly encourage you to explore it.**

Perhaps start with some reading. Here are three incredible books that completely changed my perspective on alcohol:

1. *This Naked Mind* by Annie Grace
2. *Quit Like a Woman* by Holly Whitaker
3. *We Are the Luckiest* by Laura McKowen

Or maybe try replacing drinking with something else enticing. The key here is to reduce the number of steps for decision or distraction between you and the new habit. So:

- **If knowing alcohol is in your home always tempts you,** get it out of sight! Put it in the basement or garage, dump it out, or give it to a friend.

- **If you want to sip tea or warm lemon water tonight,** then today, set out your favorite mug with your tea/lemon next to it.

- **If you want to go for a walk after dinner,** set your shoes and socks by the door, set an alarm, or schedule it with someone. (Moving your body and/or being in nature is wildly helpful in quenching a craving.)

- **If you love the ritual of holding a wine glass,** just replace what goes in it! Buy some sparkling water today. Maybe throw some lemons or limes in your cart or some lavender syrup. Jazz it up. Get *excited* for it.

EACH NO
TO DRINKING
IS A BIG
yes
TO LIFE

LAURA MCKOWEN

Here's something else that might help:

Ditch the notion that not drinking is deprivation. Instead, focus on what you're gifting yourself in the process of not poisoning yourself:

clarity? energy? vibrance? nourishment? time? joy? connection?

To help you hone in, I invite you to write specific examples of what you'd gain by saying, "Not today, booze." Is it more focused time with your child/ren? Better workouts in the morning? Increased energy to slay that dream?

If alcohol isn't a thing for you but something else is, I'm leaving the line blank. Maybe it's sugar, TV, overworking, overcommitting, or a toxic relationship. What's taking up too much space in your life?

Put it on the line, baby. Then...imagine ALL the goodness you'd be letting IN by letting that one thing GO.

BY SAYING NO TO:

_____

I'M SAYING YES TO:

_____   _____

_____   _____

_____   _____

_____   _____

LOG THE LAUGHS 17

There's nothing quite like being in the middle of a packed grocery store aisle and having your toddler randomly yell out:

"MOMMY, YOU FAH-TED!"

For the record, I didn't fart that day. (Believe me. I always take credit for my farts!) What I DID do, however, was laugh so hard...

...just like the day JeeWoo decided to pull down his pants and pee on the playground after school. When I gave him permission to take care of this emergency, I thought he'd run behind the temp building and swindle a butt-covered, standup-pee like his buddy usually did.

NOPE. Not that day.

J-Dub so innocently and very spontaneously just went for it, out in the open, in front of his friend, with NO shame, while another mom and I laughed so hard *we* almost peed.

TODDLERS ARE DRAINING,
BUT OH, MY GOODNESS,
THEY ARE ALSO HI.LAR.I.OUS.

People often say, "Good thing God made babies cute." Well, let me add to that by saying, "Good thing He made toddlers funny!"

He was like, *These tired parents will need somethin' to get 'em through those crazy days. Let's have these little humans do so many comical things, their moms won't even be able to remember them all.*

But you WILL want to remember some of those golden nuggets, so the next two pages are open for just that (with a few of my recent faves to get you started). >>>

"HEAD, SHOULDERS, PENIS, TOES"

"F*CKING TAPE!!"

When they're tantrumming
and you're about to explode,
focus on their small hands.

FOCUS POCUS 18

If there ever was a week to explode, it was the one when...

...my period was awful,
...JeeWoo and I got Covid,
...we changed schools last-minute,
...my mom-in-law went to hospice care,
...my "Mommy Wrist" pain was horrendous,
...and I was attempting to start another sober streak.

But I never raged. (!!!) I'm convinced it was because of a tip I saw from parenting experts Caitlin Slavens and Chelsea Bodie, also known as @mamapsychologists on Instagram.

They say, "When you're MAD AF and about to lose it on your kids, try this: Notice your child's little hands and feet in comparison to your hands and feet."[1]

When I'm about to blow my stack, I don't usually think to take a deep breath, splash cold water on my face, speak in a softer tone, or [insert that seemingly impossible tip you've read here].

But one look at his smaller hands immediately reminds me that he's unable to reason with me or respond to me like the adult I'm expecting him to be.

This simple, quick decision to glance at his hands gives me just the context I need to regulate and reset a bit. His tiny hands remind me of his small yet rapidly changing brain. He's only in his third year of life, yet SO much is happening for him. SO much is out of his control.

He needs more grace from me, and focusing on his hands is totally a catalyst of calm for me. I hope it is for you, too.

19 LOVE CODE MODE

Gimme 5, stay alive.
Gimme 4, shut the door.
Gimme 3, let's have tea.
Gimme 2, take off a shoe.
Gimme 1, let's have fun!

Thirty-four years later, I still remember the secret handshake that my uncle and I made up.

I also remember what my mom and I would do before we said goodnight: We'd pinky swear, kiss our fingers, and tap each other's foreheads.

Sometimes at a family gathering, my dad would look at me and pull down the outer corner of his eye. I'd do it back. It was our funny way of saying lots of things without saying anything.

> ## ALL OF THESE EXCHANGES TOOK SECONDS, YET THEY'RE STILL IMPRINTED IN MY MEMORY.

Right before tucking JeeWoo in, we used to do a thumbs up, hang loose, and some knuckles. This top-secret tradition would make all of us smile, even after the most sweat-inducing, hair-pulling attempts to get Little Man to bed.

These days, the pre-slumber sendoff consists of David tossing 100 imaginary M&Ms into JeeWoo's mouth before he blows him 10 "Kit-Kat-Oreo kisses" from the door. J-Dub LOVES it.

Not only is it something that he expects (Toddlers thrive on predictability!), but it's a special invention that only he and daddy share. It's their thang. It's their unspoken code for "I love you."

What about you? Are you recalling things from your own childhood or reminded of what you already do with your kiddo/s? Perhaps you're inspired to add some magic to a mundane routine.

Wherever you land in Love Code Mode, I hope these tiny traditions melt you into the moment each time they're acted out.

the things we remember forever
have a context that's familiar
+ something a 'lil peculiar

So, THIS explains why I'll never forget:

- The nickel my uncle would playfully demand from me every time I passed him in his favorite seat.
- The password my friend Jessica and I had to say (CC11892) when we climbed into the magical transportation to fairyland (her mom's green van).
- That pinky-swear-forehead-kiss routine my mom and I had.

All of these moments had a slightly peculiar twist.

According to Per Sederberg, a psychology professor at The Ohio State University who's spent his career studying memory:

"You have to build a memory on the scaffolding of what you already know, but then you have to violate the expectations somewhat. It has to be a little bit weird."[1]

So, the next time you're:

...being too hard on yourself,
...bogged down by big expectations,
...or struggling with the daily, mundane motions of being a mom:

Don't forget that a little a dash of magic
or a sprinkle of the unexpected
can go a really long way.

Before I became a mom:
I was terrified of germs.

Now, I'm that person who:
Sees her kid's donut do an icing-side
face plant in the middle of a coffee
shop floor, picks it up, gives it a quick
glance, and hands it back to him.

Turns out:
Mamas are always growing, too.

MEASURE YOUR GROWTH 20

Your turn! Before you became a mom, what were you afraid of that you have now overcome or no longer think twice about? What did you say you would never do, but now you do it, and you're proud of it, find freedom in it, or just *get* it?

List three ways you've grown:

Before I became a mom:

1

2

3

Now, I'm that person who:

1

2

3

TINY TIME CAPSULE **21**

I still haven't started that memory book for JeeWoo. Not really sure why. (Time? Emotions? Toddler?) But I'd still like to document some things NOT on social media that he can read and savor someday.

If ya feel me, and you're looking for something that won't take much time but will still be super meaningful, try this:

Write down 10 simple memories,
seal them up, and save 'em for later.

Don't overthink this. Take a sheet of paper and jot down 10 joyful moments (big and small). Similar to the Happy Memory Study in "Glass Canvas" on page 65, think things that sparked emotion, captured the senses, or harnessed the power of firsts.

Here's what came to mind with JeeWoo:

- "Feeling the plane land the day we brought you home."
- "That giraffe stuffy we mailed you that you still carry everywhere."
- "Spending hours finding rolie polies with you."

FOR THE SEALING:
Put it in an envelope, bottle, jar, wrapped box, etc. (Oh! And if you do a jar or box, you could keep adding to it like a piggy bank of memories!)

FOR THE SAVING:
Do you want them to open this alone or with you? Do you want to save it till they can read or when they're 20? Whatever your wishes are, put that on the outside. Then, hide this tiny time capsule in a secret place and wait for that special day.

In the meantime, pay attention to shifts in your mindset. The sheer act of reflecting on yesterday's joyful moments just might make you more patient and present today.

22 RICE TO THE RESCUE

At the tail end of a longgg day, I was touched out, talked out, and just plain burnt out. Right before I started clawing at the walls, something in my back pocket came to the rescue:

Rice!

RICE PLAY IS ONE OF THE EASIEST, CHEAPEST WAYS TO SAVE. THE. DAY.

Here's all you need to do:

1. Pour those day-saving grains into a small box or bin. Lay a towel or blanket beneath it. (You'll thank me later.) Or if it's nice out, take this party outdoors.
2. Grab a few toys, spoons, or tools to get your toddler started.
3. Watch as their imagination explodes with ideas.

JeeWoo gets SO into this. He runs back and forth gathering cars, rocks, cups, and *all the things* while I sift the rice through my fingers and feel like I'm playing with sand on the beach.

Don't have rice? Try beans.

(IF you use rice and have dogs, be sure to clean it up when you're done. One mom's pups ate all the rice and got the runs. Oopsy poopsy!)

When they get into a zone, tip-toe away and enjoy a little recharge time. Every time I do this, I get at least an hour to catch up on something or, ya know, scroll Instagram and listen to Marco Polos.

AND: Rest assured that this sanity-saving activity has a million benefits.

Okay, not a million, but close. When your kid plays with rice, it:

- enhances memory.
- activates all five senses.
- creates a sense of calm.
- stimulates brain growth.
- ignites their imagination.
- promotes practical life skills.
- strengthens fine motor skills.
- encourages problem-solving.
- develops hand-eye coordination.[1]

And on the crazy off-chance that's not enough to blow your kid's mind, here are three ways to make their senses dance with wonder:

1: **Add some essential oils.** Try a drop or two of lavender or any skin-safe, yummy oil you've got.

2: **Make rainbow rice.** Search this term online, and you'll soon learn why moms call this their secret weapon. (I have yet to try it. You've got to have gel food coloring, time + desire to bake it, and so on, but SO MANY MOMS swear by it. Kids LOVE it.)

3: **Add sound.** Depending where their imagination takes them, add some relevant, relaxing background noise. Are they camping? Play some crackling fire. Are they at the beach? Play ocean sounds. On a safari? Get those birds chirping! Just be sure to play what YOU would find relaxing, too.

If these additions feel overwhelming, ignore them! Simply putting rice in a bowl with a few cups will be *just* enough.

"There are no seven wonders of the world in the eyes of a child. There are seven million."

—*Walt Streightiff*

LIGHT UP THE MOMENT **23**

One cold, winter night, after the hubs had been out of town for four days, I was spent once dinner hit. I wasn't in the mood to sit next to JeeWoo for yet another non-riveting meal with no convo.

Seeking a change of pace, I sat across from him and lit a little candle. Suddenly, the atmosphere changed. It became a little date for us. We smiled. He spoke! It even made our ho-hum soup feel fancy. You see...

Just the sheer act of lighting ONE candle (even if it only burns for five seconds because toddler) can immediately shift our moods, soothe our minds, and calm the chaos.

In fact, studies show that the rituals we perform before eating or drinking — saying a prayer, giving a toast, tapping a spoon against a teacup, or lighting candles — can affect our whole experience. Not only can it make something more memorable, but it can also enhance our taste buds.[1]

Perhaps this is why the 'ol birthday ritual is savored as much as it is. If it weren't for the candles, would the cake be as special? Would a wish even be made? Would we be as inclined to take pictures and videos?

Are these fleeting flames that powerful? Is it really that simple? I'm sure sold. In fact, here's something that might work some magic:

PUT A BIRTHDAY CANDLE ON <u>ANYTHING</u> AND SING "HAPPY MORNING TO YOU."

I've done this with a muffin, banana, and cookie, and not only has J-Dub LOVED it, but it sure has lightened some particularly heavy mornings.

So, mama...

Don't wait till a birthday or even a good day to light a tiny, mighty fire. EVERY day is worth celebrating, and candles change everything.

PEARS ON THE STAIRS 24

JeeWoo and I have this thing where any time we both eat a pear, we have to enjoy them on the stairs together. I'm not quite sure how this little ritual began (#mombrain), but what I *do* know is that it fills us both up. Here's why:

NO ELECTRONICS

I'm not against screens. Without the shiny things, I'd never be able to cook or clean. ☺ But we all know how important it is to take a break from those addicting devices, and one of the best ways to do it? Out of sight, out of mind.

By removing ourselves from the kitchen table (where I often let my phone tag along) and the living room (where a big 'ol rectangle on the wall lures us in), we have none of our usual digital distractions. We have no choice but to focus on our food and each other, which brings me to the next benefit:

ALL THE SENSORY DELIGHTS

When you sit next to a toddler in a place that feels like the middle of nowhere, while tightly gripping to and loudly gnawing on a ripe piece of fruit, all of your senses come alive.

What would normally be a passive, rushed, or on-the-move snack sesh suddenly becomes a slowed-down, full-blown, mind-body experience. Not only does it allow for a nice recharge, but it also promotes...

HEALTHIER BELLIES + HAPPIER BRAINS

Studies show that mindful eating can help us digest better, derive more pleasure from what we're grubbin' on, recognize when we're full (which is so important for littles!), and avoid emotional or stress eating. It can make us feel fuller quicker and satisfied longer.[1]

Most importantly, snacking unplugged with your little one is...

AN OPPORTUNITY FOR CONNECTION

I think JeeWoo runs for those stairs when we've got our pears because he knows he'll have all of me. Even if we're not talking, we're saying all the loving things to each other just by being oh-so-presently hip to hip.

So, when your mini eating machine needs their 76th snack of the day, why not make it for two and create a nourishing tradition to boot?

>>> No pears? No Stairs? No Problem!

Perhaps have a mini, no-frills picnic in a random location, like:

- under the table.
- on the kitchen floor.
- in the middle of a fort.
- [insert your random spot here].

As long as you're both replenishing in an offbeat location or away from a screen, your mission is complete. Bon Appetit!

recap

Did you follow suit with some stairs 'n' fruit or did you start your own tradition? Dish it!

JEEWOO RUNS
FOR THOSE STAIRS
WHEN WE'VE
GOT OUR PEARS
BECAUSE HE
KNOWS HE'LL
HAVE ALL OF ME.

25 LEAD THE WAY

"I just can't play Barbies all day."
"Playing pretend isn't in my wheelhouse."
"I don't have patience for crafts and messes."

Maybe some of these words feel familiar to you. Or maybe you thrive in playtime, but this week, you're burnt out and *plum out* of all things imaginative.

Well, my tired yet joy-seeking mama, here's a prompt that might save the day: Think of what YOU love, and lead the way!

Sometimes (keyword: sometimes), I find that if I initiate what JeeWoo and I do, especially if it's something *I* enjoy, he'll feed off my energy and love it, too.

This takes a little creativity and a lot of letting go of what your normal go-tos would be, because ain't no toddler's gonna hang through any chatting on phones, playing of instruments, writing in journals, or [insert soul-feeding activity that was once uninterrupted here].

But over time, I've found great success with the following:

- pumping up the music and working out together.
- inviting him to help me in the garden.
- dancing in the kitchen.

With daddy, I've seen him thrive when:

- football is on. (He feels David's excitement + wants to be part of it.)
- anything needs fixing. (He loves a good mystery.)
- anything needs assembling. (He LIVES to build things.)

I find that when I make it a special occasion / announce it / invite him before we begin, it usually turns out to be a win-win.

Me: JeeWooooo! I have a very special project I need your help with!
JW: Yessss??!!
Me: Let's...clip...roses...together!
JW: YAYYYYYY!

Make that small thing BIG from the start,
and you'll likely have their little heart.

ME: I can't believe that in the span of three hours, I got nothing accomplished besides
doing nothing.

HUBS: That's still an accomplishment.

DO NOTHING 26

When I know a solid break is coming or I'll have a silent house to myself for a bit, I salivate over how I'll seize my time.

From focused writing or uninterrupted piano playing to a long shower or catching up on *Emily in Paris*, my mental list is long and dreamy.

But then I GET that time, and all I can often do is sit and scroll my phone, sit and stare, or lie in the middle of the floor. And almost every time I do this, I feel guilty.

> **It's hard not to let shame creep in when you're not doing anything. But sometimes doing nothing is everything you need to do.**

According to a 2022 study in the *Journal of Experimental Psychology*, those who make time to sit on their butt and do nothing actually enjoy it more than expected and are more likely to be better at problem-solving and thinking in new ways.[1]

I mean, some of the most revolutionary inventions and creative works of our time weren't birthed from focused moments. They were born out of daydreams and leisure time. (Einstein's Theory of Relativity. The plot of *Harry Potter*. Gmail. Newton's Law of Gravity.)

But you don't need to become an inventor or be radically inspired to know that this is doing your brain and body good. Yes, all you may think about is what better things you could be doing, but don't worry for one second. Accept it ALL for what it is, because on the other side of this so-called "wasted time," you WILL be less stressed and more energized.

So, mama, here's your permission to do, well, *nothing.* ENJOY IT!

curlers.
warm chocolate.
PB + cinnamon toast.

BIG-LITTLE LOVE ACTS **27**

♥ If she hadn't already braided my hair the night before, my mom would put curlers in my hair every morning.

♥ If my hot chocolate was too hot, my dad would stand outside with it until it was "warm chocolate."

♥ Before we'd watch *The Price is Right*, my grandma would make me peanut butter and cinnamon toast.

Those are the things I so vividly remember. They were predictable. They were consistent. They made me feel loved.

SO. Don't underestimate the power of simple, repeated acts of service for your kids. They're working more magic than you think!

remember

What big-little things did your people do for you?

recap

What big-little things do you do for your kid/s?

TRASH TO TREASURE 28

"JeeWooooooo! It's dinner tiiiime!" I announced with a paper towel roll one night. THE. LOOK. ON. HIS. FACE.

For the first time in history, something broke his attention from *Grizzy and the Lemmings* on the first try. He came RUNNING with the biggest smile and hopped right up to the table.

As the night went on, it was fun to watch him take this piece of trash and transform it into 1,432 treasures. From a telescope and monster tail to a microphone and gas station pump, the kid found countless ways to play with a long, hollow piece of cardboard.

When it came time for bedtime, brushing teeth, and all the things that often feel like *pulling* teeth, this prized paper tube came in handy yet again.

"JeeWoooooo, it's time to use your flosssssserrrrrr!"
"JeeWooooo, put on your shirt, pleeeeease!"

Not only was he super happy, but he was also obedient. (What?!)

THIS OH-SO-GIGGLY, EXTRA LOTION-Y, STRONGER-THAN-STRONG-WILLED CHILD WAS ACTUALLY LISTENING TO ME.

Isn't it incredible how a simple task can be completely transformed for a toddler when you make it FUN? Toss in a piece of trash and even more excitement will unfold.

Every time I hand this boy a piece of almost-garbage or another empty box, he acts like I've given him GOLD.

You should've seen him when daddy was cleaning out the junk drawer. He sat on the floor like he was in the first row of the most riveting show. As David attempted to toss dimes, rubber bands, old pens, and pizza coupons into the trash, our little pirate blocked his shots, sniped the junk, and added to his pile of riches.

Oh, toddlers. They're master upcyclers!

So, the next time you're about to let go of that no-longer-needed thing, remember: One mom's trash is another toddler's treasure.

recap

What rubbish has your kid flipped into something marvelous? Did that empty Pringles can save the day? Did that egg carton spark connection AND self-play?

remember

What trash did you turn to treasure when you were little? (My favorite part about pizza delivery was that my Barbies got a new coffee table. All hail the pizza saver!)

ONE MOM'S
TRASH
is
ANOTHER TODDLER'S
treasure

29 SNEAK A CHEEK KISS

It was day three of JeeWoo being home and we were tiiired. Thanks to a lovely thing called jet lag, the little dude got up at 3 a.m. and *stayed* up.

After 76 waking hours and 34 tantrums, it was somehow only 9 a.m. So, there we were...sitting on the floor against the kitchen cabinets, still in our pajamas, and wondering what the heck was happening. He was sitting in a pile of crumbs from his 17th snack and spilling milk on himself. I was on my 92nd cup of coffee and watching the spillage in slow motion.

Then, on a whim, I did something that was new for us: I kissed his cheek. And his immediate smile washed away all of my overwhelm.

Everything just...changed.

You see, when we show our kids affection, not only does it release happy hormones, increase attachment, regulate emotions, and help their bodies and brains grow,[1] but here's my favorite part: It makes the world stop.

Nothing slows down time more than a kiss on the cheek, especially if it's unexpected.

Ahem! A surprise cheek smooch from JeeWoo was the genesis of Mama Be Present, remember? That spontaneous sliver of connection spurred an entire passion project around savoring tiny moments. If that's not magic, I don't know what is.

Speaking of magic, sometimes while I'm cooking and JeeWoo's watching his shows, I'll walk over to the couch, hang my face in front of his, and plant one on his cheek. Everything stops again. Even if it's been the hardest day ever, I ALWAYS have energy for this.

So, mama. Want to show your kiddo you love 'em in an instant or create a special memory on the spot? Go ahead...

Sneak a cheek kiss.

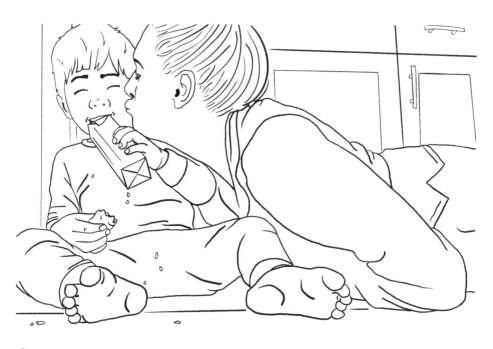

you're gonna miss this
you're gonna miss this
you're gonna miss this
you're gonna miss this
you're gonna miss this
you're gonna miss this
you're gonna miss this
you're gonna miss this
you're gonna miss this

FLIP THE PERSPECTIVE

One morning, as I walked into the bathroom, JeeWoo fell apart on the floor because I didn't invite him. When I sat on the toilet, he oh-so-conveniently squeezed himself between my knees and wailed.

"You need an assist?" David yelled, as he came back for his keys.

"All good up here!" I replied, as I hugged Bugaboo so tight.

Just when I thought he couldn't get any louder, he started yelling, "DADDY! STAAAAY!"

The consoling continued, as I told him that daddy had to go to work. What happened next was so ridiculous, I didn't know if I should laugh or cry:

"Mommy, itch my arm," thy toddler demanded, as we both looked at the patch of skin he was more than capable of tackling. But, of course, I itched his arm, and all I could think was: *You're gonna miss this.*

What are some things you currently find comically ridiculous, irritating, or intense about raising a toddler? Write them below:

As I write this, JeeWoo and David are downstairs watching soccer. Or, well, David's *trying* to watch soccer while J-Dub does everything he can to interrupt: continual questions. endless stories. constant n-o-i-s-e.

Right now, I find this annoying. But deep in my bones, I know I will miss this. It reminds me of what Brené Brown once said regarding her research on joy and gratitude:

"When I interview people who went through horrific things — the loss of children, genocide, violence, trauma — and I ask, 'What's the hardest loss?' They never talk about the extraordinary things. They say:

'I miss the the ordinary moments. I miss hearing the screen door slam and knowing my husband's home from work. I miss hearing my kids fighting in the backyard. I miss the way that my wife set the table.'"[1]

When something is over, our memory is flooded with what unwittingly gripped our senses, unknowingly brought us comfort, and secretly helped us grow.

That said, let's try something:

> 1: Pretend it's 20 years from now. What you wrote down has disappeared. It's never coming back. You no longer need to tend to your child's every need. Your house is clean and quiet.
>
> 2: Now, look back at your list and circle what you miss.
>
> 3: If you couldn't circle anything today (which is totally okay!), or new things are coming to mind, write them below:

"Only with distance from the minute-to-minute anxieties of caring for a small child does its sweeping beauty come into full view. But this isn't so much a shortcoming of youth as it is a gift of age. Hindsight allows us to put suffering into context and recognize the purpose it served in our lives."

—*Stephanie H. Murray*

31 SNAP A MENTAL PIC

One morning, I actually googled "How to be a present mom when you're burnt out." While glazing over tip after tiring tip on how to fight "mommy burnout," one mom's perspective caught my weary eye.

As Vicki Glembocki wrote about how watching her little girl run to the bus stop made her smile, and how in that moment, she wasn't thinking about anything else, I felt like I was right there with her. I could see her daughter's "little bum" wiggling side to side under her giant backpack.[1]

Her tip, to notice when you're already being mindful, really stuck with me. It got me thinking about the power of paying attention *in snippets*.

When we catch ourselves being attentive, even in the most fleeting of moments, there's a certain kind of magic at work. The kind that makes us present. The kind that brings us back to life.

No matter how tired you are, zeroing in on something with your senses — even for a few juicy seconds — is more than doable. The ripple effects are remarkable.

Later that morning, JeeWoo knocked me down on the ground and started pecking at my chin with his nose. As I busted out laughing, I took a mental picture. I pretended like there was a camera in my brain and when I blinked, I forever documented the scene. This split-second decision pulled me into the moment and lifted my mood.

During lunchtime, we had a little picnic in front of the TV. While gnawing on a carrot and transfixed on the screen, J-Dub reached over and locked arms with mine.

<click> I captured that, too.

While carrying him from the shopping cart to the car one day, I thought about how big he's getting and how one of these days, I won't be able to carry him anymore. As I held him tightly, I tucked my face into his neck, and <click> melted into it all.

During bath time that night, he was extra joyful and giggly. <click>

Snapping mental pics has quickly become a little habit that has sweetened many situations. Not only is it oh-so-accessible, but it also has this way of making the impossible feel possible again. It takes everyday moments of your life and turns them into vivid vignettes to remember...

...all in the blink of an eye.

"We had so much fun,
I forgot to take pictures."

I see this on social media a lot, and I love it. It always reminds me that the best times are the ones that aren't documented.

Think back to some of your most vivid memories. Do you have pictures of those exact moments? Probably not.

Of course, without pictures, there are so many times in our lives we would forget. It's sooo much fun to flip back and scroll back in time. But here's the thing:

When you're constantly trying to capture things with a camera, you're impacting your memory of them.

Linda Henkel, a professor of psychology at Fairfield University, studied this exact phenomenon. In an experiment with a group of undergrads at a museum, she asked them to take pictures of some objects and simply observe others.

The next day, she asked the students certain details about the objects. It was clear that they remembered less about the things they photographed and more about the things they merely observed.[2]

According to her, when we take a picture, we're relying on the camera to remember for us. We're not engaging in the mental processing that would allow us to recall these moments.

Now, she's not anti-camera. She agrees that taking pictures can help free up mental space for other stuff, and of course, help us recall certain things. The problem is when we overdo it to the point that we don't take *any* time to fully immerse ourselves in an experience.

So, here's your reminder to put down your phone and open your eyes and ears.

Perhaps try going an entire day without taking pictures. Soak in the moment, or hey, take some mental pics instead.

See what "clicks." ☺

get ready for a
game-changing
scrub-a-dub-dub

GLOW STICK DIP **32**

Remember when I told you that you wouldn't have to buy anything for these joy prompts except maybe some glow sticks? Well, here we are.

If you don't have a box of these things on the ready, stop what you're doing and order 'em already!

Then, when an invite to bath time brings The Toddler Wrath,
ask 'em the following:

HOW 'BOUT A GLOW STICK BATH?

Their tears will subside. Their frown will fade away.
Then, oh-so-enthusiastically, they'll shout the loudest YAAAAAY!

Perhaps this is a trick you've used time and again,
Or maybe you're like, Whoa! Toddler Rave Bath for the WIN!

Wherever you're at, here's something to agree on:
Everything's more fun with a little bit of NEON!

And oh, the joy that can spark,
When things glow in the dark!

**So, flick off the lights, drop the sticks in the tub,
And get ready for a game-changing scrub-a-dub-dub.**

From bracelets and swords to crowns and necklaces,
With these bendy wonder wands, the possibilities are endless.

So the next time your moods could use a good flip,
Don't forget the power of a GLOW STICK DIP!

grow through what
you go through

#TBGB 33

Whenever I'm in the thick of a challenging time, it often helps to focus on a **Throwback Growth Bout**. What the heck is that, you ask?

It's my silly, coined way of saying to look back in time and see how you've grown. It means to reflect on something that felt hard while you were in it, but revealed beauty to you on the other side. #TBGB

Was there a specific time in your life that made you open your eyes so wide that you were grateful for the struggle?

Think:

- that whole friggin' season that slowly prepared you for [insert beautiful thing here].
- those couple of days of illness that gave you a newfound appreciation for [something of the senses here].
- those 10 straight hours of [x] that led you to [y], or, or, or.

Don't overthink it.

Go with what first comes to mind, and on the next two pages, let your thoughts spill onto the page.

Then, take a few moments to revel in your resilience.

**Let your words serve as a glimmer of hope.
Let them remind you of how much you've
grown and will continue to grow.**

Let them show you that you've got this,
and you WILL get through this again.

Remember when you thought you couldn't
learn to drive? go to college? run the race?
wait for the adoption? have the baby?
live with the grief? give the speech?
lift the weights? survive the day?

And then you did?

Do that again.

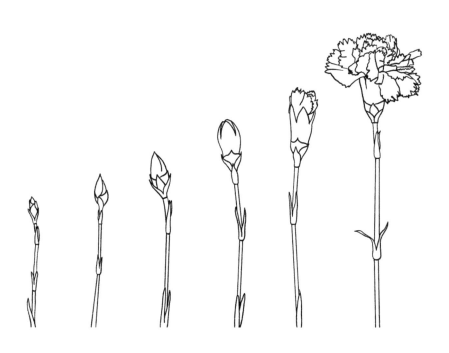

34 LET 'EM LEAD

It often feels like toddlers "rule the roost," but if you recount a whole day, these vulnerable, ultimately clueless humans don't have much say. Perhaps they need a breather from hearing:

"Hang on, sweetie, let me finish this text." "Mommy needs to make coffee first." "Not right now, bud. We need to get dressed."

Of course, there's nothing wrong with boundaries, structure, cleanliness, and all the things that make the world go 'round. But:

How many times a day are we blocking their invites or ideas because they're inconvenient / annoying / not in our imaginative wheelhouse?

No matter how badly you want to avoid playing *their* way, going *their* speed, or letting *them* take charge, remember this:

> **When we allow kids to call the shots, not only
> are we strengthening our connection to them,
> but we're helping them build confidence to lead
> and communicate. We're giving them respect.**

SO, when they invite you, join them. And when things get painfully repetitive, slow, or boring, don't divert them to something else. Follow their lead. Fake it till you make it.

Pretend you're an actress. Pretend you're trying out for "Mom of the Year." Give 'em everything you've got. Get so into it that you lose yourself in it. Put yourself so deep in your kid's shoes that you have absolutely no time to lose. They will LOVE you for it.

And who knows? Maybe this silly, once-avoided thing is exactly what you need. So, pause your to-dos, open your mind, and let. them. lead.

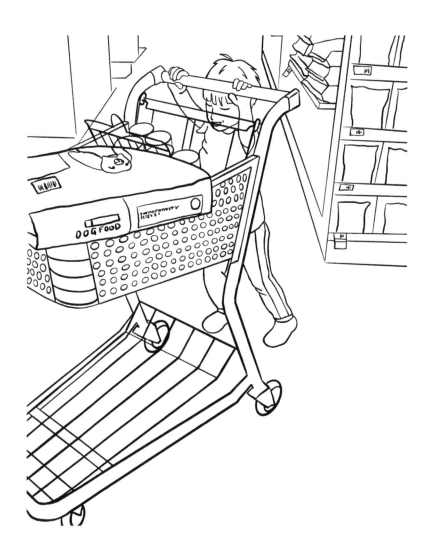

Letting a toddler lead isn't just about joining them in their playful pursuits.

It's also about respecting their unique timeline of development and trusting that they're exactly where they need to be.

Did you know that it can take anywhere from five days to three years for a moth or butterfly to emerge from their chrysalis?

The ones that take their time aren't just dilly-dallying for the heck of it. They aren't doing this to drive their parents crazy. Their instincts are telling them to wait for rain or better living conditions.

This natural process is a helpful reminder in this season of life. I often get caught up in JeeWoo's timing with various milestones and wonder why he's not on track with this or that. But who's to say there's even a TRACK?

We get frustrated if they're not potty trained, swimming, speaking clearly, or knowing every letter by a certain point. We forget that these small humans know exactly who they are and have their own schedules, personalities, thoughts, and comfort levels.

Just like no snowflake or fingerprint
is the same, no toddler is either.

So, no matter how hard it may be to see little to no movement with certain things, try this joyful approach:

Let go, mama. They'll get there. And when they do, it'll be perfect timing.

Is there something you've been struggling to let happen in its own time? How could you let go?

FLASHLIGHTS AND WHISPERS 35

Some days, we get home dangerously close to nap time, and all I can think about is how hard the transition will be. Other days, we've got all the time in the world and JeeWoo's just not having it.

In those desperate moments, here's something that's worked some serious magic:

Grabbing a flashlight and starting to whisper.

One time, we grabbed two flashlights and looked for monsters for a few minutes before seamlessly slipping into his room for the 'ol nap routine. We whispered the whole way, and he listened the whole time. (I've never seen him so willing to put on a Pull-up!)

Another time, we flipped on my phone's flashlight, ventured into a dark bathroom, and made shadow puppets on the wall before another round of painless nap prep.

Yesterday, with just *minutes* to spare, I said, "JeeWoo, two minutes till nap time. Should we read books with flashlights, today?"

"YESSSSSSS!" he yelled.

"Okay, then. We can ONLY whisper," I said with a soft voice, as he quickly followed suit.

This tactic has worked many times like a dream. It has even made that book I've read 1,000 times feel like the first time. So, if you're in a nap- or bed-time pinch or needing a day-saving trick, I hope this switch of the senses works for you, too!

Or here's something else you could do...

Not in the mood to read
that same 32-page book to
your kid for the millionth
time this week?

Read it in a New York accent.

It'll change everything.

ADD AN ACCENT 36

I tawlked like dis wit *Duh Powt-Powt Fish in duh Big-Big Dawhk* aahnd I was SOH into it. I had noh dee-sigh-yuh tuh sum-muh-rize oh skip duh pay-ges. Nawt like I do dat oh any-ding, aw-rite?

Just in case my attempt at putting a New York accent to paper was a complete failure:

I said that the second I added an accent to *The Pout-Pout Fish in the Big-Big Dark*, I got so into it. I had no desire to even summarize or skip the pages. (Not like I do that or anything.) It's crazy, though:

JUST ONE TINY SHIFT IN MY ACTIONS COMPLETELY CHANGED HOW I SHOWED UP.

Even though I was exhausted, I was enjoying myself and not rushing through the book. And JeeWoo could totally feel it. He loved it.

Now, you obviously don't have to hail from Brooklyn. Be British if you want, or try rapping through the book. Just change. it. up.

And the next time they're not complying with brushing their teeth, putting on shoes, or whatever they're refusing to do, add an accent then, too! (Want to *really* up the ante? Sing your requests in opera.)

Not in a place to be silly? Just make it a game.

Take a task and accentuate it with a little competition or imagination.

- Turn leaving the house into "prepping to board a spaceship."
- Turn teeth-brushing into "killing the sugar monsters."
- Turn heading upstairs into a "race for the gold."

Who knows? You just might start a new tradition!

JUST TRY IT 37

"Mommy, need help!" JeeWoo shouted.
"Buddy, what are you even trying to do?" I asked.
"Hang truck here!" he yelled, as he motioned to a light switch out of reach.
"Oh, buddy, your truck won't hang there."
"Mommy! Need help!"
"Bud! It's not gonna hang from there!"
"Mom! Help!"
"Okay, okay, I'll try it. I'll SHOW you how it can't hang from there."

I tried. It worked. My mind was blown. A week later, I heard:

"Mom, help!" This time, he was trying to attach his juice cup to the diaper bag dispenser and hang THAT from a light switch.

"Buddy, that's definitely not going to hang there," I said.
"Mommm! Try!"

I tried...again. It worked...again. Mind blown...again.

Here's the lesson those tiny, mighty toggles taught me:

Stop assuming something can't happen.
Start believing it can. Just try it!

In other words...

- Maybe that transition from nap time to solo quiet time will go better than you think.
- Perhaps that second attempt at potty training won't be as disastrous as the first.

- Maybe they'll do better in full-day preschool than expected.
- So, they didn't thrive in soccer, swimming, OR gymnastics. Maybe karate or JiuJitsu is where it's at!
- What if they CAN carry that chair up the stairs over their head?

RE: chair, this actually happened one day. J-Dub kept insisting, so I followed closely behind him, and he never needed my help. What?!

It got me wondering:

What ELSE could be happening
if I simply believed it could?

What are some things you've been putting off or simply saying no to because you *think* it will be a struggle or you *think* it won't work?

Write 'em down:

Then, take some sage advice from that adventurous toddler of yours and just try it. Try *one*.

Yes, it might fail miserably, but you'll try again and/or LEARN something.

Remember! There's a reason FAIL has so many acronyms. (First Attempt in Learning. First Attempt Isn't (the) Last. Focus Attention Into Learning.) It's all a beautiful part of the process.

Or what if, just what if, it works out better than you ever imagined? You'll never know until you try!

What if...

...it works out
better than you
ever imagined?

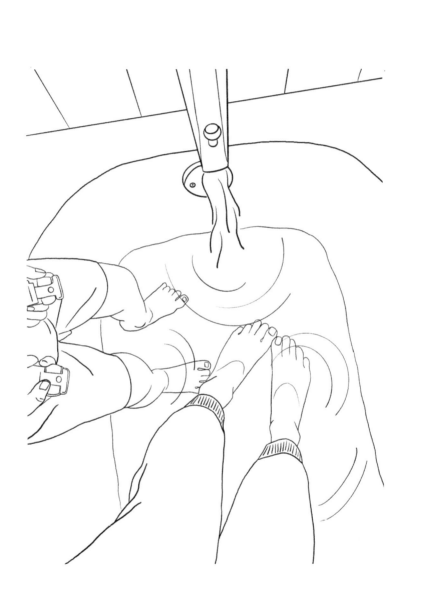

TREAT YOUR FEET 38

Are you...

...cold?
...tired?
...anxious?
...stressed?
...getting sick?
...feeling any pain?

Well, simply dipping your feet into warm water for 10-15 minutes will do wonders. (If you're kid-free, increase the temperature and the benefits will, too.)[1]

Not only will your toddler LOVE an impromptu invite to an aquatic adventure, but this treat for your feet will likely lift your mood.

Anddd the heat will increase your circulation, giving you some extra energy to boot.

Every time we do this, JeeWoo quickly loses his clothes and finds ALL the toys to bring in the water. While he has a blast, I get to chill, and afterwards, we both feel refreshed.

Bada bing,
bada BOOM!

So...

Whether you fill some of the tub or bust out a bucket, I promise you, a spontaneous foot soak WILL knock your socks off!

PARTNER IN PLAY CRIME 39

After a long afternoon of errands, emergency bathroom stops, and all those comical mishaps that come with a toddler in tow, JeeWoo and I were hangry, tired, and stuck in traffic. I needed a flip in perspective, and I needed it FAST.

When "Down Under" by Men at Work came on, I pumped up the volume and did some silly dancing in my seat. The goal was to shake off the crazies and make JeeWoo smile. THAT, I accomplished.

What I didn't intend for? The trucker on my left to see me. Even though he was laughing, I was embarrassed. But it got me thinking: If I were alone, would I have danced like that? No way! Then, I had an AHA:

Raising a toddler means having a 24/7 wingman for all your wildest, be-a-kid-again cravings. Kiddos are ALWAYS waiting in the wings to roll down hills, swing on swings, hang upside down, and do silly things.

If there's something you want to do, but it feels pointless, petty, or like something you'd never dare do solo, NOW is the time to embrace the ultimate partner in play crime: your TODDLER!

What playful things are coming to mind? Give 'em life below:

Even if you're rolling your eyes or have no energy right now, dig into your daydreams and put a ditty (or three) in your back pocket. Need a little inspo? Perhaps try:

Handing flowers out to strangers

Not long after I put this in writing, JeeWoo and I did this! Right when we got to the grocery store, we bought a simple bundle of daisies and handed them out while we shopped. Every single person was so surprised. The checker told us that we made a LOT of people's day! (Psst! Prefer something a little more introverted? Maybe leave little notes or Post-its in random spots in the store.)

Blowing bubbles in a random place

I have often thought about handing bubbles to a homeless person, blowing bubbles from a bench in a busy park, or setting up a bubble machine in a high-traffic spot. I have yet to try it, but now that JeeWoo's in my life, I have some extra courage.

Surprising someone with sidewalk chalk

On the mornings my mom-in-law had chemo, J-Dub and I would sneak over to her driveway and decorate it with sidewalk chalk. She loved seeing it. We loved leaving it. (Not feeling artsy? Why not draw a hopscotch somewhere? See who partakes!)

Sending a trucker salute

Want to turn trash day into a special occasion or add some excitement to your time on the road? When you see a truck-a trekkin', get those arms-a pumpin', and get those horns-a honkin'! See-a what-a happens.

[your adventure here]

If none of this is jiving with you or feels too forced, that's OKAY! Sometimes the best things are the spontaneous, unplanned things. So, keep an eye out for those special opportunities. You will KNOW when it's high time for a play crime!

RAISING A TODDLER
MEANS HAVING A
24/7 WINGMAN
FOR SPONTANEOUS
ADVENTURE

BIT BY BIT
LITTLE BY LITTLE
SLOWLY BUT SURELY
SHE RETURNED TO HERSELF

RETURN TO YOU 40

Just a few months after starting **Mama Be Present**, I was struggling. I couldn't tell if my thyroid had plummeted, if depression was creeping in, or if I was burnt out from JeeWoo no longer sleeping in. But losing my morning quiet time to write, create, and be with me (and only me) was surely making me crazy.

When I told my mom I was about to see my old therapist, she said:

"I have a feeling you don't need to go sit and talk. I think you need something for YOU. Maybe take piano lessons or go play some golf. Do something that'll make you laugh."

Now, don't get me wrong about therapy. I firmly believe in it and have deeply benefited from it in similar seasons. But at that particular time, my mom knew what I personally needed.

There was only one problem:

I HAD NO CLUE WHAT THAT THING FOR ME EVEN WAS ANYMORE.

I even had to ask for ideas in a Facebook Group with local moms. Over sixty suggestions later, there was one thing that ignited something in me: standup comedy classes.

Just the *thought* of this brought me back to an old part of me and reminded me of one of my favorite seasons.

It was a time of uncertainty, as I had just nixed a move to New York for graphic design school (Thanks, recession!) and was between jobs. But I was traveling some, golfing more, blogging for a new startup, and going to open mic stand-up every Tuesday night.

I had no idea what I was doing, but I just remember feeling so free, rebellious, rested, and adventurous. So adventurous, I did my own stand-up routine one night.

How'd it go? Let me just say that I didn't show my face at the Squire Lounge for a year, and when I returned, the bartender remembered me. The proof? His impression of my impression of Bobcat Goldthwait.

I'm glad someone remembers that night, because thanks to huge nerves, going second to last, and having too much time to drink who-knows-how-many vodka sodas, the only thing I recall is the emcee motioning for me to wrap it up and me, well, not wrapping it up.

Needless to say, I bombed. But fourteen years later, two friends say this is one of their favorite memories ever. It's one of mine, too. Yep, something I can't literally remember stands out in my mind, because:

IT WASN'T JUST ABOUT THE STAND-UP. IT WAS ABOUT DOING SOMETHING COURAGEOUS AND NEW.

It was about getting everyone in that room to pay more attention to a woman, no matter how ridiculous she was, and hopefully inspiring someone else to think, *If SHE can do this, I can do this, too.*

It was about the freedom of it all. Getting on a stage and throwing away all the judgements and pressure of society is quite liberating, I must say.

After that hilarious flashback to my mid-20s, I thought it was time to redeem myself and at least be consciously aware of how my dad jokes and shoddy impressions are received.

But as I looked into classes, nothing tugged at me. I wasn't about to be downtown till 10 p.m. on a Wednesday (#momlife) or commit four hours of my Saturdays, which are often prime time for Brit time. #daddyshome

In my hunt for stand-up classes, I realized, yet again, that it wasn't about the actual stand-up. It was more about the desire to feel like I used to:

spontaneous. seen. silly. joyful. free.

So, I started seeking out those core desires in small, accessible ways, like...

- Cracking jokes on the "stage of life" in posts, texts, and conversations.
- Being goofy with the best partner in play crime: JeeWoo!
- Waking up earlier so I could create solo and feel free.
- Spontaneously posting dance videos.
- Playing the piano...and sharing it.

AND BIT BY BIT, I CAME BACK ALIVE.

But just like every child is different, so is every mom.

- Maybe you need something more focused and consistent, like yoga every Monday night.
- Or maybe the simple yet life-changing act of journaling is calling your name.
- Perhaps a solo stay in a hotel with room service and nine episodes of *Workin' Moms* is just what'll recharge you.
- Maybe talking to someone is what you need most, but you can't make it across town or don't feel like putting real pants on. (There are tons of great online therapy services these days, like BetterHelp, Talkspace, and more.)

Or what about being fully away from home, every single week, for more than an hour, and honing a totally new skill? That's exactly what helped Mary McConville, illustrator behind **Grow Up Brite Creations**, feel like herself again.

When her kids were younger, she wasn't quite sure what she wanted to do, but something kept bringing her back to art. So, she asked her husband if he could be home at a specific time so she could go have three uninterrupted hours at art class once a week.

For two years, she learned all things watercolor. Then, she discovered digital illustration, and since 2018, she's been connecting with moms all over the world through her art online.

Her relatable illustrations with encouraging quotes are like a big 'ol hug through the screen. They capture the real moments of motherhood while helping every mom feel seen.

She also has this incredible ability to see beauty in the hard times — especially the ones when we forget who we are.

"I think this happens a lot with moms," she says. "It's normal. It's inevitable. But that's when you really start to think, *What is it that's really going to make me happy?* It gives you that push to do it."

It's like you have to get totally overwhelmed by motherhood to propel yourself out of it and find what you love.

If you're in this phase right now, I hope these stories get your wheels turning again. I hope they keep you holding on. And remember:

"It's OKAY to get lost in motherhood and be in a funk," says Mary. "Because right when you're in the worst of it is right before it's going to get much better."

remember

When was the last time you felt truly free and full of joy?

Is there something you did as a kid that you no longer do because someone said you weren't good enough / it feels self-indulgent / life got busy?

realize

Are there scenarios / dreams / hobbies that creep
into your daydreams but feel petty or pointless?

Of all you wrote down, what's pulling at you the most?

reignite

How could you bring this thing (or the feelings
associated with this thing) back into your life?

What's something you could do in 10 minutes TODAY
that would inch you closer to this thing?

where from here?

If you enjoyed this journey and don't want it to end either, here are some ways we can keep the goodness going:

staying connected

WRITE ME // Want to share something that sparked from the book? Have an AHA-mazing idea? Need a safe place to vent? I'd love to hear from you: **brit@britstueven.com**.

LET'S FOLLOW EACH OTHER // If you're on Instagram, you can find me at **@mamabepresent** and **@britstueven**.

JOIN THE COMMUNITY // If you're on Facebook, join the convo and coffee-clinking at **facebook.com/groups/mamabepresent**.

1:1 accountability

On many of the self-care prompts, we barely scratched the surface. If you desire deeper brainstorming, further accountability, and/or custom ideas on *anything* that's tugging at you, I'm HERE for you.

I've worked 1:1 with people in all kinds of formats: in-person coffee chats, over the phone, on Marco Polo, and even exclusively via text + email. Let's see what works best for you, yeah?

Find more info at **britstueven.com/1-on-1-coaching**.

programs + events

I have many dreams (and things in the works!) for **Mama Be Present** programs + gatherings. From book clubs to online journeys to quarterly events, the possibilities are endless.

To stay abreast on ways to participate, sign up for my email list at **bit.ly/NotesFromBrit** or find more info at **britstueven.com**.

sources

Chapter 1 - Say Eye Love You

1. Leong, Victoria, "Eye contact with your baby helps synchronise your brainwaves," *University of Cambridge*, November 9, 2017, https://www.cam.ac.uk/research/news/eye-contact-with-your-baby-helps-synchronise-your-brainwaves.

Chapter 5 - Hide Your Phone

1: Adrian F. Ward, Kristen Duke, Ayelet Gneezy, and Maarten W. Bos, "Brain Drain: The Mere Presence of One's Own Smartphone Reduces Available Cognitive Capacity," *Journal of the Association for Consumer Research*, 2017, 2:2, 140-154, https://doi.org/10.1086/691462.

Chapter 6 - Just Roll With It

1: Kelcie McKenney, "Why Music Changes Your Mood SO Dramatically (And How to Make it Work for You)," *Healthista*, November 11, 2014, https://www.healthista.com/music-mood.

2: Dr. David and Amanda Erickson (@flourishinghomesandfamilies), "Five Brain Benefits of a Daily Dance Party," Instagram post, Dec 28, 2022, https://www.instagram.com/p/CmtvBKbJooS.

Chapter 8 - Stop. Drop. Breathe.

1: Ling Beisecker, "The Holistic Benefits of Savasana," *Do You*, August 19, 2016, https://www.doyou.com/the-holistic-benefits-of-savasana-57950.

Chapter 9 - Greet 'Em Grinning

1: Ronald E. Riggio Ph.D., "There's Magic in Your Smile: How Smiling Affects Your Brain," *Psychology Today*, June 25, 2012, https://www.psychologytoday.com/us/blog/cutting-edge-leadership/201206/there-s-magic-in-your-smile.

Chapter 12 - Glass Canvas

1: Wiking, Meik, *The Art of Making Memories: How to Create and Remember Happy Moments*, United Kingdom: Penguin Random House UK, 2019.

Chapter 14 - A Love Note to You

1: Kross, E., Bruehlman-Senecal E., Park, J., Burson, A., Dougherty, A., Shablack, H., Bremner, R., Moser, J., & Ayduk, O., "Self-Talk as a Regulatory Mechanism: How You Do It Matters," Journal of Personality and Social Psychology, 2014, 106 (2): 304-24, https://doi.org/10.1037/a0035173.

Chapter 18 - Focus Pocus

1: Parenting & Postpartum Experts (@mamapsychologists), "When you're MAD AF...Try This." Instagram post, July 6, 2022, https://www.instagram.com/p/Cm9jxR1JDqy.

Chapter 19 - Love Code Mode

1: Ohio State News, "Why the Peculiar Stands Out in Our Memory," June 19, 2017, https://news.osu.edu/why-the-peculiar-stands-out-in-our-memory.

Chapter 22 - Rice to the Rescue

1: Nicole Smith, "Sensory Rice Play," *The Eco Kind*, March 24, 2022, https://theecokind.com/blogs/news/sensory-rice-play.

Chapter 23 - Light Up The Moment

1: Yajin Wang, Francesca Gino, and Michael Norton, "To Savor the Flavor, Perform a Short Ritual First," *Association for Psychological Science*, July 22, 2013, https://www.psychologicalscience.org/news/releases/to-savor-the-flavor-perform-a-short-ritual-first.html.

Chapter 24 - Pears on the Stairs

1: Harvard School of Public Health, "Mindful Eating," accessed February 10, 2023, https://www.hsph.harvard.edu/nutritionsource/mindful-eating.

Chapter 26 - Do Nothing

1: Aya Hatano, Cansu Ogulmus, Hiroaki Shigemasu, and Kou Murayama, "Thinking About Thinking: People Underestimate How Enjoyable and Engaging Just Waiting is," *Journal of Experimental Psychology: General*, Epub July 28, 2022, https://doi.org/10.1037/xge0001255.

Chapter 29 - Sneak a Cheek Kiss

1: Pamela Li, "The Importance Of Hugging Your Child & 7 Amazing Benefits," *Parenting For Brain*, January 19, 2023, https://www.parentingforbrain.com/children-hugging.

Chapter 30 - Flip the Perspective

1: Brené Brown, "SuperSoul Sunday: Dr. Brené Brown on Joy: It's Terrifying," interview by Oprah Winfrey, *SuperSoul Sunday*, Oprah Winfrey Network, video, 5:07-5:33. https://www.youtube.com/watch?v=RKV0BWSPfOw&t=17s.

2: Stephanie H. Murray, "Why We Long For the Most Difficult Days of Parenthood," *The Atlantic*, October 19, 2022, https://www.theatlantic.com/family/archive/2022/10/early-child-parenting-first-years-hardest/671790.

Chapter 31 - Snap a Mental Pic

1: Vicki Glembocki, "6 Simple Ways to Be a More Present Parent," *Parents*, May 8, 2020, https://www.parents.com/parenting/better-parenting/advice/simple-ways-to-be-a-more-present-parent.

2: Manoush Zomorodi, *Bored and Brilliant: How Spacing Out Can Unlock Your Most Productive and Creative Self*, St. Martin's Press, 2017.

Chapter 38 - Treat Your Feet

1: Kambra Clifford, "The Healing Benefits of Foot Baths: Beyond Ultimate Tranquility," Foot Files, accessed February 10, 2023, https://www.footfiles.com/wellness/foot-baths/article/the-healing-benefits-of-foot-baths-beyond-ultimate-tranquility.

thank you

Thank you, God, for giving me courage to *finally* create a book.

Thank you, David, for your patience and countless pep talks in this process. Thank you for always supporting my dreams. You're an amazing partner in parenting. Where would I be without you? (Definitely not laughing as much!) Ich liebe dich.

Thank you, JeeWoo, for making me a mama (your Forever Mama!), for teaching me about joy, for joining me in all the adventures I waited so long to take with you, and showing me full-circle magic every single day. You're my buddy.

Thank you, Mama (Deb) and Daddio (Mark), for giving me life, constant love, and oh-so-fond memories. Thank you for always seeing me. Thank you for always believing in me and responding with ALL the hearts and applause emojis to any writing I've ever sent you. Thank you for loving on our Cutie Boy!

Thank you, Nicole, for all of your encouragement, honesty, and help my whole life. Your ability to show up for others never ceases to amaze me. I'm grateful you're my sister. I hope you know what an incredible mom you are.

Thank you, Momo (Colleen) and Papa (Gary), for raising the incredible man I'm married to. Thank you for everything you've done for us and seen in us. Dad 2, your replies to my newsletters mean more than you know. Momo, thank you for always telling me I'm a writer. We miss you so much it hurts.

Thank you, everyone in my family, for your constant love. I'm grateful for and inspired by every single one of you — near, far, and no longer with us.

Thank you, Jerry, for ev.er.y.thing. You're a great friend. You booked your flight for the launch before the book was even finished. (!!!) You're beyond talented. Your illustrations brought this thing to LIFE. Creating with you was pure joy. Love you.

Thank you, Mama Be Present Community, for your open minds and honest hearts. Special thanks to Erin, Sarah, Kristal, Amy, Beret, Sariah, and Christin for ALL of your thoughtful feedback and impactful participation.

Thank you, dearest women in my life, for encouraging and inspiring me always: Kate, Adi, Mirna, Jen, Brandee, Kaitlin, Katie, Amy, Jodi, Alicia, Kendra, Cari, Liz, Eunice, Karlynn, Ashley, Lizzie, Lana, Olivia, Robin, Loraye, Gaylynn, Sara, Andrea, Mel, Leslie, Kelli, Nancy, Ursla, Sarah, Priyanka, Meghann, and so many more.

Thank you, dear reader, for being here. I truly hope this inspired you.

CPSIA information can be obtained
at www.ICGtesting.com
Printed in the USA
BVHW051217050623
665408BV00002B/8